AMERICAN FURNITURE

see figure 155

AMERICAN FURNITURE

UNDERSTANDING
STYLES, CONSTRUCTION, AND QUALITY

JOHN T. KIRK

HARRY N. ABRAMS, INC., PUBLISHERS
NEW YORK

This book is dedicated to the memory of Derek Shrub and
Danny Robbins and to a friendship with Dick Albright.

Contents

Dating by Styles

Urban Work

In major urban centers, each style overlapped the next by about five years. There were a few instances when an urban high-style maker introduced a new style earlier, or continued it later, than the general date blocks.

Seventeenth Century	1635–1705
Earlier	1635–1650
Later	1650–1705
William and Mary	1700–1730
Queen Anne	1725–1760
Chippendale	1750–1790
Federal	1785–1835
Neoclassical	1785–1830
Greco-Roman	1805–1835

Rural Work

In areas less directly influenced by European changes, each style, or feature of a style, remained an option for decades after a new one was introduced.

Mixed Styles

When a cabinetmaker mixed two or more readily identifiable style features in one work, it is easy to date the work by the latest one. For example, the neoclassical-style brasses on the Chippendale-style chest-on-chest in figure 167 place it after 1770. Dating by the latest feature can be more difficult when a maker kept alive an old-fashioned idea but altered it to work with a newer taste. The oval-top table in figure 72 has the actively shaped skirt rails, legs, feet, and stretchers popular during William and Mary styling. About a half century later, the creator of figure 228 took the idea of an oval top above splayed legs and made a visual statement compatible with the new streamlined neoclassical style of about 1800.

Acknowledgments

The material in this book was presented in its most extended form during courses I taught at Boston University and in a condensed manner during lectures for the Sotheby's American Arts Course, New York. During most of the years I taught at Sotheby's, the program was directed by Betsy Garrett, who made the visits enjoyable. On occasion, she had me further condense the ideas and issues into a one-and-one-half-hour introductory lecture during collectors' weekends she held at museums. It was after one of these "How to Look at American Furniture" lectures that the idea of the book burst full blown into view: "I could do that—look sequentially at big issues while talking about beauty, fakes, and collecting"—in a book that would feel like an enjoyable series of slide lectures.

The production of a book is a complicated process that involves many people. Margaret Kaplan at Abrams, with friendly energy, encouraged the project; without her determination it would not have been written and I thank her. For decades I have taken American furniture very seriously, but I have always wanted to stand aside from any over-reverence of the material. I thank Ed Marquand for designing a book that captures both the seriousness and the freewheeling quality I wanted to introduce. It was a pleasure to work with Christina Gimlin, Vivian Larkins, and Marie Weiler at Marquand Books, Inc. Beautiful new photographs by Paul Macapia and Michael Fredericks added to the pleasure of including unpublished material.

During the two years I studied furniture design in Denmark, furniture architect Rigmore Andersen began the honing of my eye by routinely asking, "Which of these pieces is better?" Virginia and Bagley Wright's quizzing me about just how good is the eight-million-dollar-plus Christopher Townsend desk and bookcase (figures 190 and 191) caused me to develop the section on the three very expensive Newport pieces. Virginia Wright's inquisitiveness about whether Queen Anne chairs were the first instance of a dual role for negative and positive spaces encouraged a reaching back to that idea's origin in China. Jane Garrett was my project developer at Alfred A. Knopf when some of the ideas, developed further here, first appeared in print. Lance Mayer reviewed the discussion of painting and staining maple to make it appear as walnut or mahogany, and Tom Denenberg advised on the Wallace Nutting section. I am pleased that Gerry Ward, with his vast knowledge of American objects and the relevant literature, was able to serve as the editor. Sue Bartlett entered various versions of the manuscript into the computer. Kathi Drummy entered the captions and notes and made revisions to the manuscript. Others who contributed in a variety of ways were Dick Albright, Terry Albright, Katie Bates, Lisa Becker, Susan Buck, Ralph Carpenter, Wendy Cooper, Nancy Evans, Dean Failey, Betsy Garrett, Jerry Grant, Stephen Gray, Tanya Hayes, Bill Hosley, Rock Hushka, Jan Hwang, Brock Jobe, Tom Johnson, Karen Keane, Leslie Keno, Al Klyberg, Sharon Koomler, Tom Kugelman, Jack Lindsey, David Martin, Pam McClusky, Susan Montgomery, Robert Mussey, Jane Prentiss, Bill Rathbun, Albert Sack, Robert Sack, Bill Stahl, Mike Whitt, Nan Wolverton, Dominic Zambito, and Philip Zea.

The book is dedicated to three people who have affected my professional and everyday life. Derek Shrub developed the first auction-house-based Works of Art Course, at Sotheby's, London. He had the rare eye that could look at and judge quality and visual relationships in everything from ancient Chinese artifacts to Pop Art while passing with great wisdom through French and English furniture. Danny Robbins got me to look at contemporary art by suggesting a trade: he would teach me about contemporary works, and I would teach him about American furniture. In contemporary art I have found the same involvement of the maker's hand and mind, interest in surfaces and forms, and influences of outside forces that furniture had long ago awakened. Dick Albright continues a dialogue that often touches on early furniture, but the relationship is about friendship.

Without the support, guidance, and wisdom of Trevor Fairbrother, life would be quite plain.

John T. Kirk
Seattle, Washington, 2000

INTRODUCTION

This book is about beauty. It seeks to understand how beauty was created, and demonstrates the art of perceiving what was put there for the viewer. In addition there is encouragement to value the patina that time and use have added. A piece of early furniture can inform us of the maker, town, or area in which it was produced, and tell us something about the cultural strata in which it was first used. We can see how an object is like or differs from other works from its home area and similar material from other regions; how it was incorporated into its first situation; and how its roles in society have changed over time. How later owners, dealers, and scholars have discussed and presented a piece informs us of changing cultural situations. All of these outside factors are touched on here, but this book is primarily about the visual enjoyment of the artifact—a primary force in why the piece was made.

Fig. 1

A Book About Looking

This is the first time I have in print moved sequentially from the seventeenth century to the glories of the Shaker aesthetic of 1800 to 1850. The text skips rapidly through the rest of the nineteenth century, the years when the machine had an ever greater role than the hand in making the final statement. I end with a brief look at Gustav Stickley as representative of the urge to let the handmade confront the machine, and, finally, there is an assessment of Wallace Nutting's importance in bringing into prominence early American furniture. How his reproductions differ from the original designs shows what was most prized in the early pieces at the beginning of the twentieth century.

The book is organized into seven parts divided into brief sections that focus on a few major pieces—simple or elaborate—and these are often accompanied by informative smaller images. I have included a number of non-furniture images, for to understand one means of artistic expression is to more easily see how the others fit into the general style sequence. There are a judicious number of European pieces, for until about 1900 American expressions closely paralleled their Old World counterparts. Placing European and American work side by side makes evident the dependence of American ex- amples while revealing the uniqueness of American statements.

In grasping what I wanted to do, Margaret Kaplan at Abrams said, "Yes, people want to know how to look at what is in a museum." Designer Ed Marquand encouraged a book that helps people look at an object they are considering buying—even when it is modestly priced and of a type made later than most of those discovered here. It helps perception if you have some knowledge of style changes to facilitate pigeonholing a piece into a time sequence. Knowledge of the variations in a form between American regions is also helpful. An awareness of the difference between similar European and American pieces is useful. But to *see* a piece is primarily to look in a detailed manner while thinking about what you see.

On the first day of teaching the introductory course on American furniture at Boston University, I assigned a paper due the second

FIG. 1 Ek Antiques, East Providence, Rhode Island, 1974.

FIG. 2

day: a visual analysis of the great cupboard that appears as figure 41.
I suggested that if the students saw nothing of interest in this very
consciously organized piece, they should use a watch, ponder what
was put there for three to five minutes, and then renew their commitment of time until the piece began to "work." Many of the papers
began, "At first I did not like it, it was too complicated"—not a surprising response from people who grew up in the era of modernism.
All of the papers progressed to a full or nearly full description of the
harmony of the basic constructional units and carefully orchestrated
decorative elements.

People have different gifts or natural instincts which condition
how they first approach a piece. Benno Forman, the gifted histor-
ian of seventeenth- and early eighteenth-century furniture, was
intuitively a "paper documents" person: he naturally began with
the written or printed word and moved from there toward the three-
dimensional artifact. He longed to know the maker, his situation,
and the manner in which the piece had been made. As a teacher in
Winterthur Museum's Program in Early American Culture, he was
a significant voice in training a legion of students. Looking at things
in a museum with him was exciting. I was most easily thrilled by an
aesthetic high or surprised by an aesthetic lapse. For example, when
looking at an early eighteenth-century tall clock with him I asked,
"Why isn't there a molding around the inner edge of the frame
holding the glass in front of the clock face? There is always a molding
there. It doesn't look right." He had not noted the absence of the
molding, which was missing because the door had been replaced.
But he knew other things I did not: the makers who had produced
the works and the case, and the business conditions in which they
had functioned. Our discussions sparkled when we interwove my
aesthetic concern and his historical knowledge. Most viewers fall

FIG. 3

FIG. 4

FIG. 3 Low-back Windsor armchair. Ek Antiques, East Providence, Rhode Island.

FIG. 4 Low-back Windsor armchair, 1750-80, Philadelphia, Pennsylvania. Woods unknown; later black paint. Courtesy, Israel Sack, Inc., New York.

between these extremes, and some think about artifacts with totally different concerns. We all need to compensate for our natural focuses by carefully considering factors that do not arise from our natural instincts.

To see is to expect to find. The illustrations in figures 1 to 3 are a later photographic record of a visit I made to an East Providence, Rhode Island, antique shop. The owner knew what he had, but he did not feel the need to isolate the pieces of the eighteenth-century Pennsylvania Windsor chair. The chair probably came apart because it had long been exposed to the weather, which deeply marked its surface. I have not seen the chair since taking the photographs, but understand it was purchased and reassembled. It must look something like the chair in figure 4, but without paint. I wonder if it was not most thrilling as it appears in figure 2, where the echoing shapes of the parts are intimate and the extreme weathering does not seem intrusive.

Contributing to the difficulty of exposing oneself to an object is the way so much early furniture is seen in publications and in domestic and institutional settings. Most people prefer experiencing an assemblage of earlier material, delighting in an "early" ambiance. The principal outlet for scholarly information before the advent of university training in the field, and the resulting scholarly journals, was *The Magazine Antiques,* which began publication in 1922. The favored series there is "Living With Antiques," where personally gathered material is displayed in "real" or more usually "in the style of" early architectural settings. Rarely can any private person or public institution arrange early furniture in its original room, and even when they can it is virtually impossible to know how the pieces were placed at any historic moment before the advent of the camera. Even then rooms were often adjusted for their photographic portraits.

FIG. 5 Port Royal Parlor, Winterthur
Museum.

FIG. 6 Installation view of raised chairs in
"Connecticut Furniture, Seventeenth and
Eighteenth Centuries" exhibition, 1967.
Wadsworth Atheneum.

The Winterthur Museum, near Wilmington, Delaware, was the
home of Henry Francis du Pont, who, with an extraordinary eye for
quality of design—from the highly styled to the plain vernacular—
and with a deep pocketbook, gathered and arranged a great collection of material in rooms he created using woodwork from an array
of early houses. Sometimes he adjusted the original parts to suit the
space he had available. Du Pont began collecting American things
early in the 1920s and became one of the most active buyers of early
material until he moved to a smaller building on his estate and made
his elegant home a public institution in 1951. In some two hundred
rooms and display areas he had arranged seventy thousand objects
and created the most exquisite late colonial revival display of American and, to him, related foreign material. The room in figure 5 is a
modern statement: in the eighteenth century, high chests of drawers
were in bedrooms, a parlor might contain a sofa, and it and the
other limited number of pieces were arranged around the edge of
the room—unless a table and chairs were pulled out for use. Most
of the floor was without a carpet. This room is a display of wonderful things arranged and used by a rich mid-twentieth-century collector. The primary reason most people visit this important museum
is not to closely inspect the objects, but to see how a very rich man
indulged his passion for living with antiques. For them the "period
room" approach makes sense.

Massing together objects of a similar date and region, possibly in
an appropriate architectural setting, does reveal similarities in form
and decoration. Placing objects as I did in the 1967 exhibition of
Connecticut furniture at the Wadsworth Atheneum (figure 6) broke
the dependence on the room setting and allowed viewers to easily see
corresponding or differing overall shapes and aspects of an object.[1]
Placing furniture on short or tall pedestals does force an awareness
of its sculptural qualities and causes some people to exclaim, "Look
at those feet," but such an arrangement obliterates any sense of how
a piece was first seen. Any display technique is but a way of grouping
and causing a dialogue between the objects, and between the objects
and the audience. As long as the pieces are not permanently glued
into place, and you can get at the things, the manner of display is
just another interesting cultural event.

What is required for perception is the desire to be vulnerable
to what is in front of you, to seek while intellectually eliminating as
much of the surroundings as you can. To see is to expect to find, and
then to say, "Yes, it works" or "No, I don't think it is that interesting
for these reasons." Then, if the piece has been sensitively displayed—
in an "early" or a modern setting—you may find relationships to
the other works nearby and to yourself. Full understanding requires
knowledge of historical influences, the maker and his community,
the first use of the piece, and how it has been perceived and understood during its progression toward your visit.

FIG. 5

FIG. 6

15

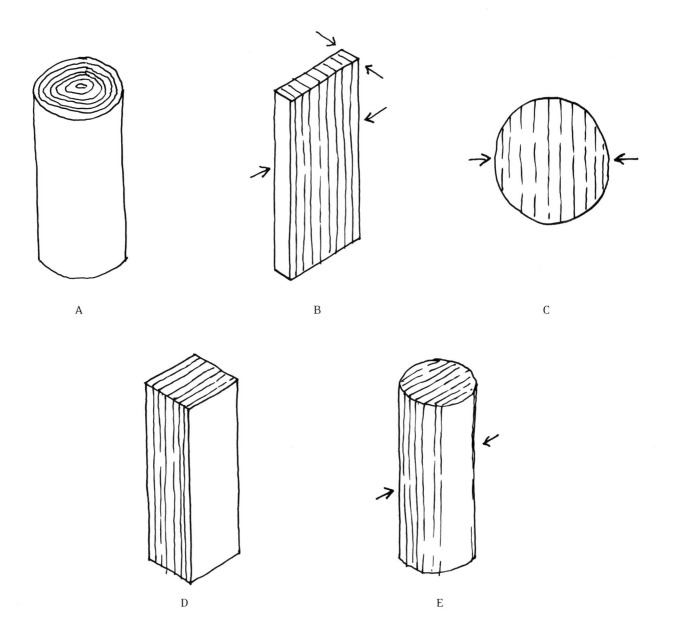

A   B   C

D   E

FIG. 7A–E

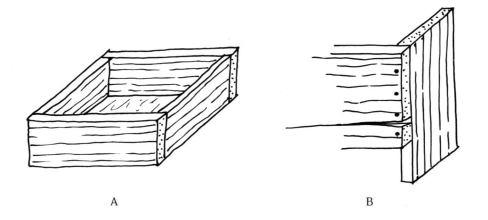

A   B

FIG. 8A–B

Wood: How It Affects Design and Signals the Authentic and the Fake

If you are anxious to look closely at spectacular furniture, skip this section. Read on, and then return here if you want to know more about shrinkage cracks and to understand the importance of color changes caused by the aging of wood, when parts are judged new because they appear inappropriate in color and surface.

Furniture is useful sculpture, and to be used it must not too radically violate the nature of its material. When a tree grows, it develops annual growth rings that denote spring and summer growth. When a board is cut from a log, the resulting piece has lines of dark, small-celled growth, running vertically, with softer cells in between (figures 7A and 7B). As the wood dries, as it seasons, more moisture leaves the soft cells and the board shrinks as indicated by the arrows. Little or no shrinkage occurs along the grain: the board does not become shorter in length. Although the majority of shrinkage takes place in the first seasoning, the board will continue to fluctuate each year as the humidity increases and decreases. This is the reason solid-wood doors stick when it is damp and become loose during dry months. Because of these changes, a circular tabletop cut from a board (or several boards glued together) will shrink during its first years to an oval as indicated in figure 7C. A three-foot-wide top may become an inch narrower in one direction than the other. (It can continue to shrink and expand up to a quarter of an inch each year unless housed in a climate-controlled environment that provides a stable relative humidity.) The slight oval of a circular top indicates age unless the shrinkage has been artificially introduced. Tubular parts of an early turned chair and the post of a stand will also become ovoid in cross section (figures 7D and 7E). Anyone thoroughly acquainted with early objects can feel with his or her hand that an old turned leg or post is now out of round. Fakers can hasten shrinkage by using heat, as we will see in Section 6.

Cabinetmakers know the propensity of wood to change, even after its first shrinkage, and this conditions their designs. Joining two boards with the grains running in the same direction—as with drawer fronts, sides, and backs (figure 8A)—allows the parts to move

FIG. 7a-e Drawings of wood shrinkage.

FIG. 8a-b Drawings of wood shrinkage.

together. If the front is of a hard wood like maple or walnut, it may move more slowly than the interior wood, which is usually a soft wood like pine, and the side boards may gain shrinkage cracks. If two wide boards are joined with their grains running in different directions (figure 8B), shrinkage cracks may appear in the fixed board. The front, back, top, and bottom boards of the chest in figure 9 run horizontally. The ends use vertical grain. If they were of horizontal grain, the feet could easily snap off through the grain. The nails that join the parts kept the front, back, and bottom firmly in place, and a shrinkage crack has appeared at the right end of the front board.

Constructing a piece of narrow parts that run in different directions, and filling the areas with panels that can seasonally move back and forth in slots in the heavier parts, greatly reduces the number of shrinkage cracks (figures 10 and 11). The splat and back stiles of a Queen Anne or Chippendale chair have vertical grain, and the grain of the crest rail runs horizontally. When the parts were assembled, there was a smooth flowing line along the edges of all the parts. As the splat and back stiles dried, the unity usually disappeared where the parts were joined (figure 12). In some cases the outer edges of the splat are too secure to move inward, and shrinkage cracks may appear in the splat.

Shrinkage as evidence of age appears in many places; one of the easiest to observe is in the mitered corners of a looking glass or picture frame. As the wood shrinks the outer points of the surrounding parts keep them from moving in, so the inner edges move toward the outer. This opens the joints (figure 13; the frame has twisted out-of-square as it dried).

FIG. 9 Six-board chest, 1650-1700, probably eastern Massachusetts. Pine; original red paint. Private collection.

18

FIG. 10

FIG. 11

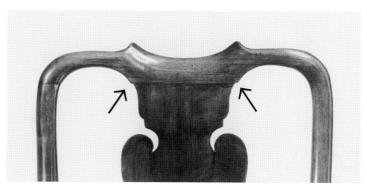

FIG. 12

FIG. 13

FIG. 10 Framed chest, 1640-80, New Haven Colony, possibly Guilford, Connecticut. White oak; red-brown paint. Yale University Art Gallery, Mabel Brady Garvan Collection.

FIG. 11 Parts of a framed chest over drawer, 1640-80, Milford, Connecticut, area. Oak. The Metropolitan Museum of Art, Gift of Mrs. Russell Sage, 1909 (10.125.27).

FIG. 12 Upper part of a chair, 1730-55, Massachusetts. Walnut. Courtesy, Israel Sack, Inc., New York.

FIG. 13 Nineteenth-century frame showing wood shrinkage.

The makers of Windsor chairs had a fine understanding of how to exploit the properties of wood. The individual parts are fashioned of the wood best suited for their shape and function. Rather than cutting through the grain of a board to make an arched top rail (as was done for the oval-back chair seen in figure 203), the chair in figure 14 has a narrow piece that was steamed to make it pliable and then bent into a circular top and extending arms. This allowed the grain to follow the curving line. After bending, a device held it in its new shape until it dried. A Windsor's seat has small drilled holes for the members of the back and larger ones for the legs. The legs have holes for the side stretchers, and the side stretchers for the medial stretcher housed into them. The holes in the seat were bored into a not-too-dry board. Very dry legs and back parts were fitted into them, and, when everything adjusted to normal room conditions, the joints became very tight. If any of the parts went all the way through the seat, they might be secured by wedges from the other side.

FIG. 14 Braced-back continuous-bow Windsor armchair, by Walter MacBride (working 1792–96 and possibly later). Maple, yellow pine, and oak; old paint. Branded "W. MACBRIDE/N-YORK." Winterthur Museum.

Windsors use with intelligence the particular qualities of different woods. The legs and the front posts under the arms are normally of maple, or another close-grain strong wood, which can be readily turned to beautiful forms without an open grain pattern. The backs are usually of woods with a springy strength such as ash or hickory. The seats are normally of a soft wood such as tulip poplar, pine, or chestnut, which is easily carved to a saddle shape. That the woods had differing colors and grain patterns did not bother the chair makers or the buyers, for the varying surfaces were obscured by a unifying paint. Its color contributed to the object's dramatic silhouette. Windsors that have been stripped of their paint show what was not meant to be seen.

The stick joint with its round members, as in Windsor chair construction, was one of the basic means of joining two pieces. The simplest and earliest way of joining wide boards was to nail them together (figure 9). The mortise-and-tenon joint (figure 11) was an early means of joining heavier members that often surround panels to create a broad surface. The thin extension, the tenon, is put into a squared hole, the mortise. After being joined, the parts were often held firm by a pin. To draw the tenon tightly into the mortise, the hole in the tenon on the rail was slightly offset from the hole in the post—it was placed slightly nearer the shoulder of the rail. The joints in figure 11 show round holes in the vertical post and oblong holes in the rails' tenons because, when the pins were driven into the offset holes, they stretched the holes in the tenons as they forced the shoulders of the rails tightly against the post.

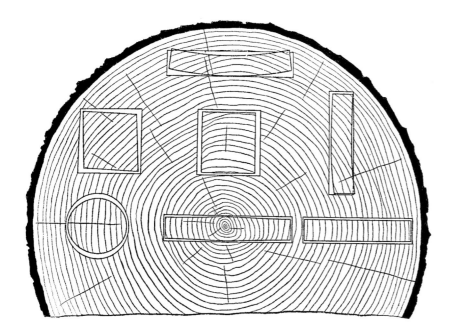

FIG. 15 Natural shrinkage of wood.

After about 1700 in this country, the creating of pieces by joining heavy members around panels gave way to creating cases out of
boards joined by dovetails. Cabinetmakers, rather than joiners,
dovetailed together the sides, top, and bottom of chests of drawers,
or the upper cases of high chests as seen in figure 62. Drawers with
fronts, backs, and sides joined by dovetails were fitted into them.

Flat boards that are not firmly held in place can warp for several
reasons: for example, where a board was taken from a log affects how
it wants to move as it dries (figure 15). Warpage also occurs when
one side of a board becomes drier than the other, and the dry side
becomes concave. This is most easily seen in double-leaf tops (as on
figures 197 and 229), when the front edge of the top leaf no longer
touches that of the lower leaf when the table is closed. A more complicated process happens to boards that are frequently wiped with a
wet cloth: the top cells are so frequently expanded by moisture that
their circular shapes become compressed into ovals (figure 16).
When the surface dries, they remain tight ovals and the board becomes cupped as seen in the leaves of figure 70.[1] Such boards can be
straightened by repeatedly wetting the convex side to turn its circular
cells into ovals while continually tightening a clamp to pull the convex side flat. Or, you can shrink with heat the convex side. I know of
one restorer who straightened warped table leaves by putting them
on the floor under a hot wood stove with the convex side up. Following the advice of another restorer/faker, I have straightened boards
with electric irons: place the cupped side down and cover the convex
side with a cloth—I used a lightweight canvas—to keep the wood from
scorching; take one or two electric irons (turn off the mister) and
dry the wood. Move the irons *very* slowly over the wood, and you will
probably see moisture rise from the wood as the board becomes flat.

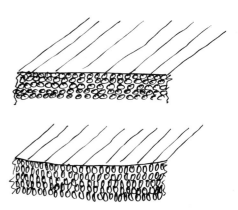

FIG. 16 Shrinkage of wood repeatedly wet
on the top surface.

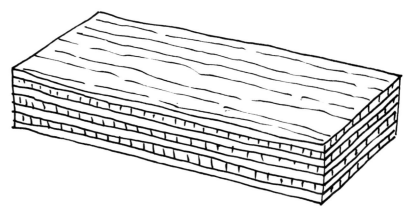

FIG. 17

I take the wood beyond straight so when I stop ironing and a normal moisture level returns, it will be straight.[2]

The center boards of drop-leaf tables with straight legs (as on figure 187) project slightly beyond their frames so when closed the leaves can drop straight toward the floor. When cabriole legs are used, the center boards project further so the leaves of closed tables clear the projecting knees. Often, the fixed center board has shrunk so much that the leaves now hit the frame or the knees and remain at an angle when down.

The movement of wood was controlled by the invention of laminated wood. It was first used extensively in Western furniture during the rococo revival of the middle of the nineteenth century (figure 242). An assemblage of thin layers of wood with their grain running in opposite directions (figure 17) is most commonly known as plywood. Each layer keeps the adjacent layers from moving. There is an odd number of layers so the grain of the outer sheets runs in the same direction, and they are of the same wood—or woods of equal strength—so one cannot impose its desire to change size. The use of seven layers in much rococo revival furniture allowed a new degree of multiple piercings, for the wood could not crack along the grain. Also, the strength of the material permitted a greater degree of high-relief carving, such as three-dimensional roses. The stability of layered woods also permits designers to create tables and other forms without an overhanging top. With plywood, or plastic, the Parsons table look can be created (figure 18).

Figures 19 to 21 show a right rear bracket foot from a mid-eighteenth-century case piece. What was originally the visible face is of horizontal-grain walnut; the back is horizontal-grain pine. A maple block with vertical grain was glued into the corner to strengthen it. The foot was attached to a case above only with glue. To provide a greater glue

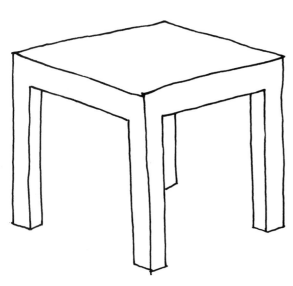

FIG. 18

FIG. 19

FIG. 20

FIG. 19 Right rear bracket foot from a case piece, 1740-1800, found in the attic of Daniel Bliss House, Rehoboth, Massachusetts. Walnut, pine, and maple; original finish. Private collection.

FIG. 20 Same as figure 19.

FIG. 21 Same as figure 19.

FIG. 21

surface, pine glue blocks were placed inside the walnut side and the pine back. You can see where the one attached to the pine back is now missing: there is a light-colored area at the top of the pine back in figures 20 and 21. Only the outside face of the walnut part received a finishing coat of varnish.

The outer face of the walnut part is the darkest area because of the color of the wood and the darkening of its varnish. If the foot had recently fallen off the case it supported, the tops of the walnut side, pine back, and pine and maple glue blocks would be light in color—like the inner corner of the foot where I have removed the maple corner glue block (figure 21). Inside the foot it is possible to see that the three woods—pine, walnut, and maple—have aged differently. But the foot still shows a unity of color and wear expected of

FIG. 22 Easy chair, 1790–1810, possibly Baltimore, Maryland. Mahogany, pine of the *taeda* group, white pine, and tulip poplar. Yale University Art Gallery, Mabel Brady Garvan Collection.

parts that have long been together, for they have been similarly exposed to air, light, dirt, and use. Any serious student of early furniture demands such unity of all surfaces.

Many pieces of furniture have had their outer surfaces refinished, which can make it difficult to judge authenticity (as we will see in Section 13). It is therefore a standard practice to look closely at those parts that were never painted or varnished, for they should show no refinishing or altering of surfaces: the interior of a chair or table, and the interior, bottom, and back of a case piece.

When upholstered furniture is for sale, it is not uncommon to see the upholstery loosened, at least that which covers the back, so viewers can judge if there is unity of color and to allow the inspection of the secondary woods (the woods not normally visible). Such woods may suggest the original place of origin, for secondary woods were almost always what was readily available locally. The presence of non-American woods, such as English pine, oak, or beech, can drastically change the monetary value of what might otherwise seem to fit into the "American look."

With a varnished rather than a painted example, the exposed wood of an upholstered piece is usually made of an expensive, fashionable wood such as walnut or mahogany. The rear legs are spliced onto an inexpensive wood to form the back stiles above the upholstery line (figure 22). On occasion, to save more money, the back legs are of a cheaper wood from floor to crest rail, and the exposed parts are stained to match the front legs. Sometimes even the rear stretcher uses a stained wood.

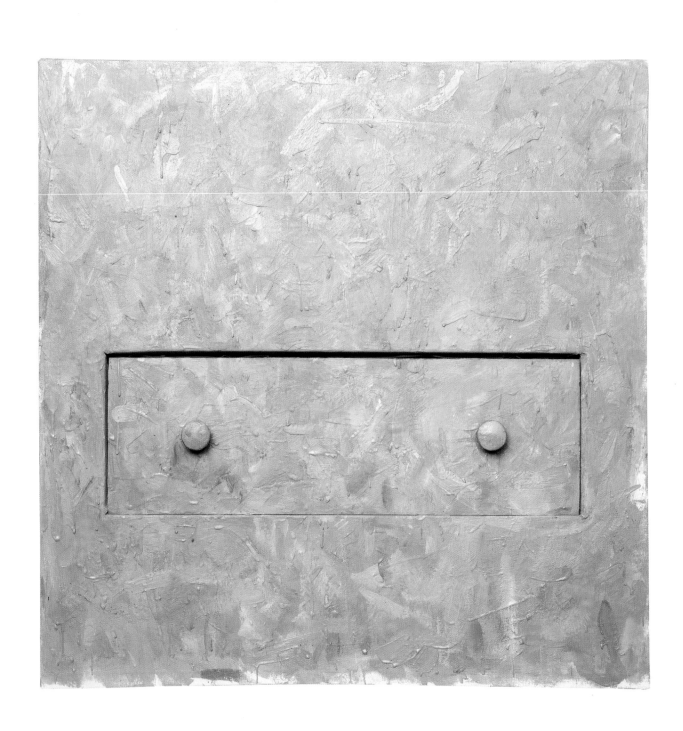

"Buy It Ratty and Leave It Alone" Revisited

In 1975, I included in my book *The Impecunious Collector's Guide to American Antiques,* a chapter titled "Buy It Ratty and Leave It Alone." I was writing particularly about painted furniture. Collectors and therefore dealers took the idea seriously, and the untouched, the grungy surface, was demanded. The term "a Kirk surface" became for a time a way to describe the condition of a piece among dealers, collectors, and furniture restorers, and even among some painting restorers.

This change to a preference for the accumulated aspect of a surface also occurred in how other early arts were treated—for example, in the enjoyment and display of "in the rough" African masks and figures. Previously, they had mostly been stripped of additions and smoothed so they fit into the modernist abstract aesthetic.[1] The growing official role in the 1970s for the ratty and heavily layered surface in part grew out of the late 1950s and 1960s preference for the instinctive, scumbled, overlaid, and often brooding works by such artists as Robert Rauschenberg and Jasper Johns (figure 23). This 1957 work is unusual for Johns in embedding a real drawer front in a canvas, but that shows his link to such "assemblage" artists as Rauschenberg. The painting has a typical scumbled Johns surface, where he used pigment in hot wax, or encaustic, to build up a layered, monochromatic, visually intriguing aspect. Seeing this kind of work intensified my commitment to leave early painted furniture untouched.[2]

In *The Impecunious Collector* I showed the illustrations included here as figures 24 and 25 and decried the condition of the first: a maple chest over two drawers which had been sanded to remove the paint—the final act of the maker—and varnished. The chest over drawer in figure 25 is very "in the rough." The top has been scrubbed free of paint, the right front foot was at some point kicked out, and the side broken above it. To hold the piece in place, a whittled wooden rod was inserted to run end to end under the drawer. One end of the rod has a knob to keep it from slipping through the hole; the other end sticks out and is held in place by an early nineteenth-century nail. For some reason, each end has an adjacent empty hole. The

FIG. 23 *The Drawer,* 1957, by Jasper Johns (b. 1930). Encaustic and assemblage on canvas. 30¾ × 30¾ in. Rose Art Museum, Brandeis University, Waltham, Massachusetts, Gervitz-Mnuchin Purchase Fund, 1963. © Jasper Johns/Licensed by VAGA, New York, N.Y.

1715–35 bat-wing brasses cover holes that once held teardrop brasses of 1700–1720. The piece has fine proportions and great visual character. Liking and wanting to live with such a piece is a particular taste. For some, the wear speaks of history. To me, this very early and well-proportioned piece is a visual delight.

The stripping of paint that began at the end of the last century was the result of several forces: from the 1880s through to the end of the second decade of the twentieth century, the arts and crafts movement reworked earlier forms while valuing the visibility of the basic materials. At the same time, there was an increased emphasis on cleanliness as new household machines and materials made the removal of dust simpler and easier-to-clean surfaces available. The collecting of early American furniture began at the end of the nineteenth century, and many of the less formal pieces had long since migrated into attics, cellars, and barns. It was consistent with prevailing social conditions that they were cleaned up before being awarded a new historical or heirloom status in homes.

The value of exposed woods became so natural that when colonial revival–style craftsmen began in the late nineteenth century to reproduce forms such as Windsor and slat-back chairs that had always been painted, they were finished not with paint but with a glossy coat of varnish that made evident the colors and grains of the various

FIG. 25 Chest over drawer, 1700–1720, New England.
Pine; original red paint; second set of brasses 1715–35.
Private collection.

woods employed (figure 245). Such a look would have been abhorred by eighteenth- and early nineteenth-century makers and buyers.

After *The Impecunious Collector* was published, I received letters from people who had loved worn pieces but knew they were pushing against the prevailing taste. A typical writer said she had always left alone what she had purchased because she loved the untouched, but that she was constantly chastised by people who wanted to know when she was going to clean up her things. Such comments spoke of the state of mind where it was judged better to permanently diminish an object, and, sadly, a written validation was needed to justify what was to her and others a natural instinct. When I showed slides of untouched painted pieces during lectures in the 1970s, at least one person in each audience would ask, "But would you like to live with it?" and I could only answer, "Oh, yes." Today, the untouched is demanded, and since the late 1970s dealers, collectors, and museums have been putting paint back onto pieces that were stripped when that look was fashionable.

The love and growing monetary worth of the ratty and the dirty soon moved from painted furniture to pieces that were highly styled and made to show expensive woods—walnut, cherry, mahogany— and, after the advent of the neoclassical taste at the end of the eighteenth century, maple. The presence of dirty varnish can help determine if parts have been changed, but on a piece designed to exhibit grain color and pattern, and finely carved detailing, it may unnecessarily reduce the intention of the maker.

The issue of what to clean is really a two-track question: painted pieces usually cannot be touched because their surfaces are like those of early bronzes, where the original surface has become pitted, encrusted, or discolored, and we now usually accept that it cannot be touched. Many painted pieces were given a coat of varnish to make them brighter and easier to clean, but, in most cases, the paint, varnish, and dirt cannot be separated and still leave a surface worth looking at. Pieces that had a clear varnish on beautiful wood to give it a glossy surface that enhanced the color of the wood can be cleaned and revarnished without diminishing the maker's final aesthetic stance. Recently, a beautiful blockfront kneehole Newport dressing table brought $3,632,500 at auction because it "retains its original patina." It is very dirty. (The piece is discussed as figure 188.)

The present high value of a dirty varnish on beautiful wood may diminish, as it has with paintings, if connoisseurs begin to want to see more clearly the maker's choice of materials and design features. Such cleaning will probably first occur on a museum-owned piece, for there the issue of resale value is removed. Probably the same outcry will ensue as when the first restorer removed from a Rembrandt much of the famous "Golden Light" by cleaning away yellowed varnish.

A piece of painted furniture valued for its beautiful surface should be left untouched and only dusted with care. Furniture that was finished only with varnish can have the surface "fed" to give it luster. Do not use a liquid, even in a spray form. You are feeding the finish, not the wood, and liquids saturate the wood after penetrating the finish; in time they turn it dark and matte, and give the piece a slightly fuzzy look. Use a good-quality paste furniture wax made without chemical additives. The traditional wax is beeswax softened in turpentine. Apply thin coats with a soft cloth. The waxy cloth may be helpful in lifting off surplus dirt. After each layer dries, buff it with a soft cloth; use a clean, soft shoe brush in any structurally complex area, such as the moldings or carvings. Prevent wax from building up thickly in recessed areas, for then its yellow color will be evident. Avoid brass cleaners that claim not to affect the wood: their chemicals, the tarnish, and particles from the brass you are rubbing will cover the wood and eventually darken it. Usually it is possible to leave the brasses on a piece when cleaning them. First protect the wood by sliding index cards behind the brasses (loosening the nuts slightly if necessary) and then proceed. If you remove the brasses, mark their backs with the location; the edges of early brasses were hand filed and they have slightly different profiles.

Ratty: A Case Study

I gave my first course as a professor at Boston University in 1975, and in the audience was a collector of contemporary paintings who thought it would be interesting to hear about American furniture. He had previously looked at early artifacts and found in the finest furniture "a great sculptural presence, particularly in the best American examples." He loved the 1960s New York school color-field paintings, especially the works by Jules Olitski and Kenneth Noland, valuing how the paint worked over broad areas of unsized canvas: the ground, the canvas, and the colors interacted in a sensitive and beautiful manner. Looking at slides and actual examples of early painted furniture, he "all of a sudden saw the true beauty and importance of patina even though it was not yet the time when patina was understood to be an essential part of beauty—the dryness of surface that makes the color itself the subject of what is being valued." A few months after he finished the course, he purchased the ball-foot chest at the left of figure 27 and the table seen in figure 33. The shallowness of the chest over two drawers makes the form tense. Its large ball-and-reel feet have great clarity of form (figure 44). The single half-round molding on the case around the drawers suggests a date of 1700–1720.

During a visit to a New Hampshire auction in 1978, he bought the blue chest (figure 26) for $300. The angled shape of its skirt dates it to the 1820s. When he was putting the chest into the car he asked, "What do I do to it?" My response was, "You just bought it because you like it, why would you do anything?" The piece has a great look: fading and wear has produced a vulnerable and visually sensitive surface. As in the surfaces of color-field paintings that focus you on both the paint and the ground, the blue paint and the pine are equal parts of the experience.

With a strict demand for exciting forms with great surfaces, the collection (figure 27) has grown to about two hundred pieces that range from the seventeenth century through a Shaker chest over two drawers. Most of them show their first coat of paint; some have a worn later coat.

FIG. 26 Six-board chest, 1820-30, New England. Pine; original blue paint. Private collection.

FIG. 27 Part of a private collection. From left: sculpture on chest over drawers by Anthony Caro, *Manifold* (1978-79); chair by Frank Lloyd Wright for the Larkin Company Administrative Building, Buffalo, New York (1904-6); painting by Joan Snyder, *Women in Camps* (1988); crucifix from New Mexico (about 1900); high chest of drawers, possibly New Hampshire (1750-80); photographic negatives with brown cross by Joseph Beuys, *Iphigenia/Titus Andronicus* (1985); gateleg table, possibly Boston, Massachusetts (1700-1735).

FIG. 29

The high chest at the center of figure 27, possibly from New Hampshire, has an immediate presence, and the shaping of the legs and feet is beautifully drawn (figure 28), not in a high-style way (as on figure 85), but with the clarity and movement of the best rural work. The brasses on the piece have not recently been polished, and it is a question among collectors as to whether the brasses on untouched painted surfaces should remain dirty. To have highly polished brasses is to set up a contrast with the worn surface: the brasses look much as they appeared when the piece was new; the painted surface does not. But to leave the brasses dirty is to diminish their role in organizing the facade where they can move the eye up the front to the cornice. To lightly clean the brasses is one solution.

The three banister-back side chairs (figure 29) play carving against turnings as their slender forms reach to their crowning top rails. Three chairs from the same set would be of greater monetary value, but joining related but dissimilar forms (figures 30 to 32) concurs with the collector's interest in contrasting great sculptural designs. The two at the left contrast urban and rural Massachusetts statements; the one at the right has fully turned legs and a crest rail placed on top of the posts.

The three tables in figures 33 to 35 contrast two styles and also the ways objects of a similar date can be quite different. The earlier William and Mary–style table plays a tight rectilinear maple frame

FIG. 29 Banister-back chairs. *Left:* 1700-1725, eastern Massachusetts, probably Boston; maple and pine; old but not original black paint; rush seat replaced with a board before black paint applied. *Center:* 1700-1730, Massachusetts, possibly Marlboro area; maple and ash; old red over black paint. *Right:* 1700-1730, middle colonies, possibly Philadelphia, Pennsylvania, or New Castle County, Delaware; maple and pine; old black paint. Private collection.

FIG. 30 Detail from left chair in figure 29.

FIG. 31 Detail from center chair in figure 29.

FIG. 32 Detail from right chair in figure 29.

FIG. 30

FIG. 31

FIG. 32

35

FIG. 33 Oval-top table, 1700–1735, eastern Massachusetts. Pine and maple; possibly original black paint. Private collection.

FIG. 34 Small table, 1730–60, from a Guilford, Connecticut, family, with the tradition that it was always the marriage breakfast table. Maple and tulip poplar; possibly original black paint. Private collection.

FIG. 33

FIG. 34

against the swing of an oval pine top; these actions are united by black paint. It does not have the drama caused by the counter thrusting lines found in the oval-top tables shown as figures 72 through 75, but it has the containment and visual force of seventeenth-century forms being rethought during the William and Mary period. The shapes of the boldly turned legs are as masterfully drawn as those on figure 70.

Awkwardness of line rarely produces a high-quality design, for it usually establishes that the maker lacked an interesting eye and technical know-how. The excitement of the small cabriole-leg table (figure 34) results from the powerfully drawn parts that are integrated into a tense rural statement: the reverse curves of the legs and skirt rails—lightened by central arches—play against the shape of the top.

Unlike the firm stances of the preceding two tables, figure 35 achieves serene beauty. The lift of the simple shaping of the skirt rails plays against the wonderful swing of the top. The turned legs have off-center turned feet that were made as demonstrated in figure 36. As seen in A, the shape was roughly sawn, and the round outline of the foot lathe turned—the points of the lathe holding the piece were in the center of the circular shape and the square at the other end. Then, B, the points were moved to the center of what would be the shaft, and the leg and the top of the foot were turned. Finally, C, the points were moved back to their original positions and the base of the foot was turned to a curving line.

The Impecunious Collector included a section that stressed the beauty of fragments of great pieces. Like heads or arms of Greek statues, a leg, finial, or crest rail can be poignantly arresting. Interesting

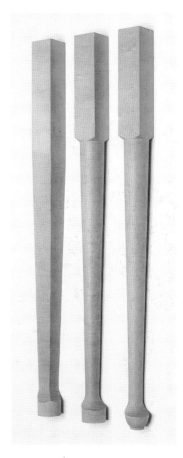

FIG. 36A–C Stages in producing turned legs with offset turned feet. The pieces were made by Tim Philbrick (b. 1952).

FIG. 35 Oval-top table, 1740–70, New England. Maple and pine; old red paint. Private collection.

fragments have become valued, and a dealer/collector recently offered $1,000 for the William and Mary turned leg (figure 63). The base of the chair from the Portsmouth area of New Hampshire (figure 37) has one of the great turned front stretchers whose outline plays thrillingly against the dramatic outline of the seat rail. Probably during the nineteenth century, when such conversions were encouraged in how-to publications, the chair (which may have had its top area heavily damaged) became a major part of a completely upholstered rocking chair: it once had a splat that fit into a slot in the lower back rail; two supporting verticals were dovetailed into that rail; the right front arm support was changed; new pieces support the center of the arms; tin bracing was added to hold the rear of the left arm; the rush-covered slip seat was replaced by a board; rockers were added; the chair was probably upholstered with a skirt hanging to the floor.

FIG. 37 Part of an armchair, original part 1740-70, related to work by the Gaines family of Portsmouth, New Hampshire. Maple; later pine seat; original red-brown paint. Private collection.

The images shown in figures 38 and 39 appeared along with figures 1 to 4 in *The Impecunious Collector,* as I encouraged a sharpness of eye when visiting congested antique shops. The collector pursued and acquired the cupboard. Since purchasing the piece, he has filled in the area of loss (at the upper left-hand corner of the open cupboard) with a temporary piece that just rests in place (figure 40). He did this to restore the outline of the tight opening in the slender vertical form. (The sides of the cupboard slant in: it is twenty-six inches across the front and twenty-two inches across the back.) Placing English eighteenth-century spotted and striped slipware in the cupboard and elsewhere is consistent with the collector's enjoyment of the interaction of related shapes, colors, and surfaces. The apples in the cupboard are renewed two or three times a year. Then they are enjoyed as "they age and develop surface interest." The six-board chest in figure 9 and the great Hadley-type chest over drawers in figure 50 are in this collection.

When I recently asked the collector why he shifted from collecting paintings to acquiring furniture, he said that part of it was "you could get something simple that was also beautiful for very little money. Paintings by great contemporary artists were so hot you had to be there when they arrived at the gallery—it was a madhouse, and expensive."

There are still modern pieces in the collection, including the Joan Snyder painting and the Frank Lloyd Wright chair in figure 27. Mostly the sensibility to form and surface is seen in the furniture, which has become personal with age.

FIG. 38

FIG. 39

FIG. 38 Ek Antiques, East Providence,
Rhode Island, 1974.

FIG. 39 Ek Antiques, East Providence,
Rhode Island, 1974.

FIG. 40 Board cupboard, eighteenth
century, found in a basement behind
pipes in Rehoboth, Massachusetts. Pine;
original red covered by early blue-gray
paint on front, sides, and front edge of
cupboard shelf. Private collection.

THE SEVENTEENTH CENTURY

The Anglo-American tradition is the main focus of this publication. Many cultures influenced American designs during the early years: the Dutch in New York state, the Germans in Pennsylvania and Texas, and the French in Louisiana, for example. In introducing related European material, my main point is to establish clearly that American designs grew out of imported ideas and visual vocabularies: people did not get off the boats when this land was being colonized and say, "Let's make American furniture." How makers on this side of the Atlantic adopted European precedents and made them appropriate to "New World" settings is indeed fascinating.

FIG. 41

Order and Integration

Medieval designs often featured carving that ran freely over the main structural parts—across rails and up posts—and elaborated panels. The Renaissance reintroduced classical order with an orchestrated use of framed rectangles, arches, columns, and organized carving. The Essex County cupboard (figure 41) may at first glance seem overly enriched with decorative features, but it and similar pieces extended into America the English version of the elaborate late Renaissance taste, also known as mannerism. It breaks a heavy mass into five horizontals: three projecting and two broad receding units. The facade is enriched by rectangles that mostly denote constructional areas. The lower two projecting bands are full-length drawers masked to appear as smaller units by applied moldings that form panels. The piece is made in two parts; the shelf above the middle drawer is the top of the lower section. The upper cupboard is held in place by tenons that go down into the lower part. The pairs of large turned columns have round tenons at each end that hold them in place; the upper ones come loose when you lift the top section.

There are six kinds of decoration: rectangular panels, arches, carvings, turnings, moldings, and paint. The arches were made on a lathe: it was rather like lathe-turning a wooden plate and keeping only the decorative rim. The resulting circle was cut in half, and each half became an arch. There are two kinds of moldings: Those that project were made on a bench with a molding plane and applied to a surface. The second type was made by the blade of a molding plane run into a main horizontal: they cross the faces of the top and bottom rails, for example. The carving continues a foliated design that emerged in antiquity. It consists of S shapes with leafy ends that are here doubled up to create heart shapes. (A more stylized version appears on the chest in figure 10.) A more linear feeling was created when the S shapes were just placed end to end.

The turnings are the most striking decorative features. They are of maple, and its hard, tight grain allowed crisp transitions between each decorative area. (Maple was not employed in English furniture of this period.) The pairs of applied turnings were made by turning

FIG. 41 Framed cupboard, 1670-1700, possibly by Emery shops, Newbury, Massachusetts, area. Oak, maple, tulip poplar, and pine. Initialed on lower doors "H/T." Museum of Fine Arts, Boston, Gift of Maurice Geeraerts in memory of Mr. and Mrs. William R. Robeson.

one unit and dividing it into two parts, and then applying the flat faces to the cupboard. How a turning was divided into two halves is not certain. To saw a slender turning in half would have been difficult, although the method was probably used for the flat spindles in banister-back chairs, as seen in figure 29, where there is rarely anything like a full half circle because of the wood lost during sawing and smoothing. The seventeenth-century practice may have been similar to what is done today: glue two pieces of maple either side of a thin soft-wood center, turn the spindle, then, with a chisel, split the piece apart through the soft center and plane away the soft wood.

The turnings may seem endlessly varied, but the basic vocabulary of seventeenth-century turned forms was limited. Originality lay in how you used the familiar. On the cupboard, the turnings employ in various ways a limited number of units—rings, reels, and ball forms—which are often joined to create baluster shapes as found in the feet. The four heavy-turned columns join with the heavy corner posts to create strong vertical front edges; they visually stop the action of the five major horizontals. Similar shapes scaled large and small play across the piece: the forms of the large balusters are repeated in miniature on their adjacent recessed areas. The final decorative feature is black paint that covers almost everything that projects and recedes.

"Read" the piece from the bottom to the top. The feet use a ring, or flattened ball, below a reel and a ring. The simulated panels on the lower drawer flank an inverted T that may once have had painted initials. The lower recessed area has paneled cupboard doors either side of a fixed area enriched with an arch; it is flanked by applied spindles. The carvings on the midlevel drawer are enclosed by moldings. (There are thin square boards with vertical grain behind each wooden knob. They bring the surface to the level of the outer edge of the moldings.) The upper recess has a central door and canted sides that lighten the upper mass and allow the eye to slip behind the freestanding columns. The upper level is the least decorated: it has only a run molding painted black. It provided a visually quiet area below what would have been a rich display of some of the family's best small objects. Paintings and inventories of houses of the period confirm that such pieces were covered by a cloth beneath pieces of pottery, silver, or glass.

There is a further integration of all this richness: two overlaid triangles. The first is formed by the three cupboard doors with the upper one as the forceful focal area. Its moldings are heavy, and the central square is turned on a point to make a diamond; the turned bosses, which are at the corners of the central squares on the lower doors, are flung out to the corners of this upper panel. The other triangular action is created by the arches: one below and two sets of paired arches above. When seen from an angle the upper arches fill

FIG. 42 Framed cupboard, 1670-1700, England. Oak. Courtesy, Phillips of Hitchin, Herts., England.

a broad area, but when viewed from the front they are foreshortened, which brings them into scale with the lower arch.

The black squares in the middle of the lower doors have incised and filled initials: "H" on the left and "T" on the right. The black paint now covers them, suggesting the paint has been freshened up sometime in the cupboard's past.

Such pieces were among the most expensive furniture forms made during the late seventeenth century, and they served both as useful, aesthetically powerful objects and as status symbols. To fully understand such a piece, think of it as having glossy black paint playing against fresh, light-colored oak, and with a display on top of a full complement of shining, expensive objects resting on a colorful cloth. It would have been in a low-ceilinged room with small windows that emitted raking light. At night, when lit by a fire, candles, or a lamp, the shining black turnings would have danced like jewels.

The English cupboard (figure 42) shows some of the features found on the American example: use of paired split spindles, turned bosses, double arches, raking sides on the top section, a more complex upper cupboard door, and black enrichment.

FIG. 43 Turned foot, 1670–1700, New England. Maple; original black paint. Formerly author's collection; stolen during a lecture.

FIG. 44 Turned foot from chest over drawers at left in figure 27, 1700–1720, probably Eastern Massachusetts. Pine and oak; original black paint. Private collection.

FIG. 43   FIG. 44

FIG. 45 Standing cup, ca. 1674, Boston, Massachusetts, by John Hull (1624–1683) and Robert Sanderson (ca. 1608–1693). Silver. Marked "RS" under rose in conforming punch and "IH" under pellets in punch curved below initials. Inscribed "Capt. Willets' donation to / ye. Ch: of Rehoboth, 1674." Yale University Art Gallery, Mabel Brady Garvan Collection.

Figures 43 and 44 show feet that were made about the same time as those on the American cupboard. The first uses maple, and the form is a tight baluster shape: the large horizontal ring or flattened ball is made to appear more horizontal by an incised ring in its outer edge. There is only a small break before it moves into a reel shape, and then again into another ring. The foot is painted black. The projecting part above the foot is the round tenon that went up into the corner post of a case piece. The oak foot (figure 44) uses the same three units but creates a volumetric form. Oak discourages smoothly integrated shapes, for its open grain produces small breaks along any sharp edge. Here there are wonderfully distinct angles between each of the three areas: the ball curves up to go a sixteenth-of-an-inch beyond the edge of the reel, then the line angles out slightly to begin the reel. The line just above the reel juts straight up to an upper ring. The round tenon is shorter than on figure 43, for it goes into the board bottom of the chest over two drawers seen at the left of figure 27.

The shapes of the cupboard's turnings and carving have a long history and appeared on a myriad of craft expressions in various media: stone, brass, silver, glass, and textiles, to name a few. The standing cup (figure 45) was made about the same time as the cupboard by the Boston silversmiths John Hull and Robert Sanderson. Like the wooden piece, the silver cup plays a decorative area of flattened ball, rings, and reels against flat and molded parts: its smooth foot is finished with a molded edge. The flat wood of the cupboard shows slight variations in its surface, for smoothness was mostly the result of planing and scraping. (Further smoothness could be achieved with

abrasives, for example: Dutch rushes [a species of horsetail], sharkskin [the older the shark, the rougher the skin], solid stones such as pumice, or various ground stones pressed into oiled leather. By 1760, sandpaper could be purchased in Boston or made in cabinetmakers' shops.[1] At least by 1800, glasspaper [ground glass glued to paper] was being used.) The slight variations in the smooth surface of the cup and foot resulted from the effects of hammering; these variations in almost smooth areas are part of what creates lively surfaces on early objects.

Although the John Coney sugar box (figure 46) shows some of the pulsating rhythms and thin legs with scroll feet of the following William and Mary period, the bands of convex lobes echo the turned bosses on the cupboard. Its lid is edged with a molding, and the punch-work texture on the center of the lid plays against the subtle smoothness found elsewhere.

FIG. 46 Sugar box, ca. 1690–1700, Boston, Massachusetts, by John Coney (1655/56-1722). Silver. Marked four times "IC" with fleur-de-lis below in heart-shaped stamp. Museum of Fine Arts, Boston, Gift of Mrs. Joseph Richmond Churchill.

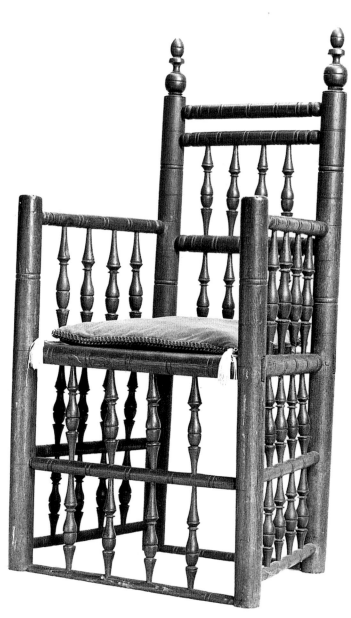

FIG. 47   FIG. 48

Which Chair Is a Fake and Why?

This section is a visual test of the ability to look closely at an object and to read both large forms and details. Answers should draw on an understanding of the turnings in the previous section. This pairing also provides an opportunity to see how true aging and wear should alter an early piece.

Questions: Which chair is early and which is new, and why is it evident from the photographs? The captions for the chairs are placed on the next page spread so readers will not too easily decide the issue.

Early in the 1970s, I saw the chair in figure 47 nestled against the giant keeping-room fireplace in the 1705 home of Ruth and Roger Bacon, which also served as their shop in Exeter, New Hampshire. The room was always visually exciting because of its changing array of interesting early material. Long before it was fashionable, Roger Bacon was a major influence on a close group of dealers as he encouraged them to leave rural pieces in the rough. He was also an important source for some private collectors such as Nina Fletcher Little. His enthusiasm for the rare and the grungy could at times override a careful analysis of a piece. My eye quickly moved on from the chair, for it was not visually exciting. I forgot the piece until I heard that the Henry Ford Museum had acquired it, and that a dealer, whom I had not represented in my 1967 Connecticut furniture exhibition, was saying that it was a fake and that I had authenticated it for the museum. Through an acquaintance I was able to visit the maker.

The chair was created in Rhode Island during the winter of 1969–70 by Armand LaMontagne, who also made rather exaggerated seventeenth-century-shaped houses with heavy overhangs. Mr. LaMontagne was happy to discuss his chair. He had decided to make a fake and get it into a major museum and then expose it, after he felt belittled by a curator during a visit to the Wallace Nutting collection of early American furniture in the Wadsworth Atheneum in Hartford, Connecticut. He made the chair out of wet oak so that it would twist as it dried. He made the big holes with an early

FIG. 47 Turned great chair, 1969-70, North Scituate, Rhode Island, by Armand LaMontagne. Oak. Henry Ford Museum and Greenfield Village.

FIG. 48 Turned great chair, 1630-55, probably Plymouth, Massachusetts. American black ash, red ash, and later white pine seat; feet and handholds missing. The new cushion is too slim to provide the proper comfort. Pilgrim Society, Plymouth, Massachusetts.

round-nosed spoon bit—which had a rounded end—and used a new bit with a flat end and a central spiral point for the small holes. If you pull the chair apart, or X-ray it, you can tell by the small holes that the chair could not have been made about 1650. But it is very rare for a museum to take a mallet and knock a chair apart, and it was not yet the standard practice to X-ray joints when questions arose.

After assembling the chair he painted it with "old porch paint," and then he knocked out two lower front spindles to suggest that they had been removed to accommodate feet. The chair received a second coat of paint before it was baked in a metal drum placed over another drum in which a fire was built. The wood shrank and twisted, the parts went out of round, and the paint coalesced. He then gave it to a "picker" in Maine who sold it to Roger Bacon, who sold it to the Ford Museum. The maker showed me the two "missing" spindles—which in themselves were not proof that he had made it—and then the "un-aged" bottom ends of the four posts, which, because their grain could be matched to the chair's posts, did prove he was the author of the chair.

I called Roger Bacon and told him what I had seen, and he tried to buy the chair back from the museum. They felt it was genuine and refused to return it. The museum published the chair on the cover of the January 1975 issue of its publication entitled *The Herald* (vol. 4, no. 1), and the maker had his revenge when he told a newspaper reporter of his achievement.

In the first place, Bacon's asking price of $9,500 was too low for such a rare form even at 1970s prices, and this should have instigated caution. More importantly, the chair does not look like a seventeenth-century chair. For example, the few early chairs of this form use four spindles in each level of the back, creating a bilateral stance (figure 48). When I asked LaMontagne why he had used three, he said it was to make the chair unique. Uniqueness of this kind often signals a faker trying to catch the eye of a collector who prizes rarity, perhaps over beauty. Rarity is never an assurance of quality. One unique fact that LaMontagne may not have known is that oak virtually never appears in early turned chairs even though it is commonly used in early framed chairs.[1]

Most evident of later work is the shape of the turnings. On some fakes, the turnings are too sharp, but here they are too mushy. The maker thought to signal age by softening the edges as though shrinkage and wear had worn them. On the genuine chair, as on the cupboard and silver pieces in Section 5, each unit of each turning is distinct. The parts of the finials of the fake flow into each other; on the old chair each section is easily discernible.

Each style period has a way of handling design, and, even with strict attention to shop practices, the eye and hand of even a careful copyist will unconsciously add some modern belief about the past

and something of the aesthetic of the time of the creation. There are many clues to understanding why figure 48 is the early chair. Like the cupboard in figure 41, and the model of a seventeenth-century house (figure 49), the early chair has a rhythmic arrangement of sticks stuck into each other, and four are slotted to hold a board seat. The parts of the chair are decorated so each echoes the enrichment of other parts and everything rises to carefully drawn finials. (The handholds on the top of the front post are missing; they would have repeated the flattened ball form found in the finials. When made, the posts would have continued some inches below the bottom stretchers as feet.)

FIG. 49 Model of the frame of a seventeenth-century house. Society for the Preservation of New England Antiquities.

The Immediate Beauty of Hadley Chests

The largest group of related very early American pieces is loosely joined under the heading Hadley chests. Examples first aroused interest in the late nineteenth century, and in 1935 Clair Franklin Luther published 108 related pieces in *The Hadley Chest.* Since then he and others have added to the list, and today about 250 related objects are known. They were made in the Hadley area of Massachusetts and other towns along the Connecticut River, from the northern edge of Massachusetts south to Enfield and Suffield, Connecticut, with some related carving executed as far south as Hartford, Connecticut.[1] More stylistically advanced pieces, like the cupboard in figure 41, required the costly features of complex attached moldings and elaborate turnings. Most of the Hadley group shows easier means of providing decorative effects.

The chest over two drawers (figure 50) is an outstanding example of a Hadley chest in untouched condition. Most examples have had their paint stripped away, and to see such a piece is to feel a greater link to the lingering medieval tradition of carving that ran freely along rails and posts. By using broad areas of paint, the creator of this piece divided the decoration into readable units. It does not have the clarified order of the cupboard seen in figure 41, but the paint did create focal areas.

The basic set of carved motifs is a scroll, a tulip, and a serrated-edge leaf. Most of these are repeated with such regularity that a template encompassing all three must have been used. The side panels have the three motifs facing both left and right. A fourth shape—a smooth-edge leaf—was carved onto the central panel. The recessed area of the carving has been textured to disguise any roughness and to set the smooth projecting parts into relief. A similar treatment of surfaces appeared on the lid of the John Coney silver sugar box in figure 46.

The posts were riven from a log, rather than sawn, saving both labor and wood. A log of at least the length of the post was stood upright, and with a froe (a stout blade with a right-angle wooden handle) wedge-shaped pieces were cleaved from it. The wedge shape

FIG. 50 Chest over two drawers, 1700-1715, Hampden County, Springfield, Massachusetts, area. Oak and pine; original red and black paint. Private collection.

FIG. 51

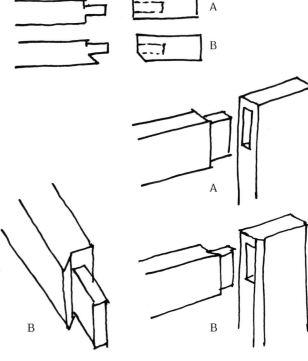

FIG. 52

of the corner posts is seen in figure 51, where the point and a "corner" of the wedge shape have been removed. Mortises were then cut
into the flattened parts to receive the tenons of the back and side
rails. (On the other three corner posts, the end grain above the tenons has not broken away and you cannot see the tenons.)

The maker used other means to shorten the time it took to make
the piece. Rather than providing complex moldings around the panels, as on figures 11 and 41, he used a plane to chamfer, or bevel,
all the rails and posts that surrounded the three front panels. This
had the advantage of producing very clean edges around the complexly carved panels. Since the bevels ran the full length of the post,
they can be seen to continue to the floor. The ends of the rails and
the drawer fronts have angled extensions (figure 52) to cover the
bevels, and those on the drawers serve as drawer stops. The English
use of chamfered parts, the four carved motifs, and the meandering
carving found on some in the Hadley chest group is seen on the
small cupboard in figure 53.[2]

While there is a sense of paint across the entire front facade of
figure 50, there is no paint in the recessed area of the carved decoration. This is because after the parts were cut to size, the edges chamfered, and the joints made, what would become the outer surfaces
were painted, and then they were carved. After all these steps, the
parts were assembled. That is why the black paint on the bevels of
the rails above and below the panels continues under the vertical
muntins (figure 54). When the piece was put together, the joints

were secured by pins. Today a maker would cover the face of the pins with paint so they would disappear into the design. On this chest, the pins were left their natural oak color (figure 54). On the sides of the piece, all the corner posts have three-unit run moldings, and their inner edges are chamfered only where they edge the panels.

Oak is not easy to carve, and the quality of the eye and hand of the carver, and the sharpness of his V-shaped chisel, is seen in the beauty of the SS initials. Close up, it is possible to discern the beginning and end of each of the curving strokes that together created an S shape.

FIG. 54 Detail from figure 50.

Related pieces that have applied moldings, turnings, and inlaid woods have been called the "best" of the Hadley chest variants, as though emulating stylistically advanced work is better. Such a comparison is like saying the portraits by the great eighteenth-century painter John Singleton Copley (figures 110, 122, and 151) are inherently "better" than equally expressive work by limners such as Rufus Hathaway, Winthrop Chandler, or Ammi Phillips (figure 226). This chest over drawers has a direct immediacy: a clarity and excitement of details that are organized to make a strong unified presence. The visual strength of the structural units is enriched by exciting carving that is clarified by paint.

Early Repainting

The paint-decorated chest over drawers (figure 55) is part of a small group of similarly enriched pieces made in the Hadley area of Massachusetts. While they continue seventeenth-century construction, which employed massive posts and rails with chamfered edges, some pieces in the group have heavy top and bottom moldings that relate them to developments in the early eighteenth century. The most famous piece in the group is a cupboard with this complex decoration and large capital letters spelling out the name of the first owner, HANNAH BARNARD. She brought the piece with her when she married John Marsh in 1715.[1]

To facilitate the laying out of the decoration, vertical and horizontal lines were cut into the center of the rails and posts. Then, using a compass with two metal points, half circles were incised along the lower three front rails to define what would become the "vines," and an array of complex circular designs were delineated on other parts. Up close, all these marks are clearly visible. The front of the chest was then coated white, and the small areas created by the incised lines decorated with a variety of colors. The white surface has lost a considerable amount of paint, flaking along the grain pattern. The more colorful areas at first appear intact, but a close look (figure 56), reveals that there are areas of loss to the white paint *under* the bright colors, although the top surfaces are intact. This is because the colorful parts are repainted, probably at the end of the nineteenth century.[2] Also, compare the quality of the colors on the chest over drawers with those on a drawer front from a related piece (figure 57). There, the colors are translucent, and the added wavy lines wiggle across the surface with a delightful freedom of movement. On figures 55 and 56, the colors are opaque and the wiggly lines stiff.

Today's restorers and fakers are much more adept at creating the look of early colors. By analyzing original paints, they can create original formulas. It remains hard, however, to make a surface look old and alive, and after about fifty years a faker's work is usually readily evident, for the later worker has added his or her concept of an earlier time, and some of their own time's artistic sensibility.

FIG. 55 Chest over two drawers, ca. 1718, Hadley, Massachusetts. Oak and pine; original white paint; other colors possibly applied in 1893. Pocumtuck Valley Memorial Association, Memorial Hall Museum, Deerfield, Massachusetts.

FIG. 56 Detail from figure 55.

The new wiggly lines move as the restorer thought seventeenth-century lines should wiggle. Or was it just carelessness? The original wavy lines on the drawer flow freely from the mind and eye of the painter, through the brush onto the surface.

FIG. 57 Detail from a chest of drawers, 1710-20,
Hadley, Massachusetts. Oak and hard pine; original
polychrome paint found under later green paint;
brasses replaced. Winterthur Museum.

THE WILLIAM AND MARY STYLE

The first style designation for American eighteenth-century furniture is named for an aesthetic stance developed in England at the end of the previous century under King William and Queen Mary II. They reigned together from 1689 to 1694, and then William ruled alone until his death in 1702. In American furniture history, the William and Mary style covers the years 1700 to 1730.

In the late seventeenth century, the architectural ordering of the Renaissance was relaxed to allow a playful movement of surfaces that broke into and projected from the basic volume. Furniture that employed this baroque classicism took considerable visual and constructional risks as it created tall forms that placed large masses on fragile arcades of baluster-shaped legs.

FIG. 58 Cabinet-on-stand, ca. 1680, Antwerp, Flanders. Ebony and other woods, tortoiseshell, ivory, floral marquetry, and ormolu. The Toledo Museum of Art, Gift of Florence Scott Libbey, 1962.

Tall and Precarious

The aristocratic cabinet-on-stand (figure 58) from Continental Europe arranges rectangular units in the case and stand and enriches them with active marquetry set into red tortoiseshell veneer. Ivory flickers around the drawer edges and is used as accents elsewhere. The front of the case around the drawers and other moldings is of cross-grooved ebony. A comparison of the legs with the similarly strict silhouette of the Dutch gentleman (figure 59) shows the unity of shape that prevailed during this style period. His symmetrically arranged cape overlaps a series of carefully orchestrated cup shapes; the feet are organized so as not to disturb the symmetry.

Like the Antwerp piece, the fashionable English cabinet-on-stand (figure 60) uses a degree of sophistication, expensive materials, and techniques not found in an American setting at this date, although many Americans were aware of such richness. (At times colonial painters gave their sitters a borrowed opulence by basing their compositions on English prints that showed people surrounded by court-level works.) It is possible to see in both of the European pieces the basic elements that were distilled to create the merchant-level London high chest of drawers (figure 61). The top of the more elaborate London piece is enriched by a complex crest flanked by finials; the cabinet is japanned in gold and silver on a ground painted to imitate tortoiseshell. The stand, like the crest, has birds holding swags. The legs pile up a series of baluster shapes; although richly carved, each layer is a readable unit. The crest and stand are silvered, and there are gilt brass mounts on the cabinet. Although much less expensive, the English merchant-level high chest (figure 61) is similar to the London cabinet-on-stand in having a complex top and a shimmering surface: the front of the drawers and the stand are veneered, and the moldings on the case use cross-banded grain. Although

FIG. 59 *Portrait of a Gentleman in Black*, 1660-70, by Gerard Terborch (1617-1681). Oil on canvas. The National Gallery, London.

FIG. 60 Cabinet-on-stand, 1680–1700, London, England. Cabinet: japanned in gold and silver on red ground painted to imitate tortoiseshell; stand and crest silvered wood; gilt brass mounts. The Victoria and Albert Museum.

FIG. 61 High chest of drawers, 1690–1710, London, England. Woods unknown. Robert Wemyss Symonds Collection of Photographs, Winterthur Library: Joseph Downs Collection of Manuscripts and Printed Ephemera.

FIG. 62 High chest of drawers, 1710-25, probably
New York, New York. Walnut and a burl veneer on
eastern white pine, walnut, soft maple, aspen, and
chestnut. Yale University Art Gallery, Mabel Brady
Garvan Collection.

FIG. 63 Leg from a dressing table, 1700-1730, Massachusetts, probably Boston. Maple; original brown paint. Private collection.

differing in their degrees of enrichment, the legs and feet of the three pieces have similar baluster shapes that create a rich movement that varies from thick to thin.

The American high chest (figure 62) does not have veneer on the top or mid-moldings, and where the similar English piece has single, cross-banded, half-round moldings on the case around the drawers, the American version uses the slightly later double half-round form.

Assigning an American piece a place of origin depends on understanding how a region created a basic mass and demands a close attention to its decorative and constructional details. This American high chest has often been catalogued as from Boston, but Benno Forman argued that it is more likely New York work. Boston pieces regularly used two short drawers in the top tier, while several documented New York pieces have three. Unlike Boston-area legs (figure 63), many New York legs have a flared support under the cup turning and a ring above the ankle baluster as found on figure 62. Many New York pieces have, as here, low-hanging paired reverse curves on the skirt and veneer panels marking the center of the case and stand. The shape of the bat-wing teardrop brasses appears on several documented New York pieces. Since brasses were imported they could also be used on Boston work, but they are not known on any documented pieces from that area.[1]

This piece is one of the great American statements of the period. The front facade of the case and the stand shimmers with burl veneer, and the drawers are edged with herringbone veneer; that richness is echoed in the solid tiger maple stretchers. The pulvinated, or bulging, lower part of the cornice covers the front of a thin drawer. The mid-molding is made in two parts: the upper half is attached to the case of drawers, the lower part to the stand. The excitement of such a piece comes in part from placing great weight on six legs that are attached to the mass only by short round tenons (as seen on figure 63). Many related pieces have little left of the original arcading. If such a piece remains intact and has not been tightened with glue, it is usually possible to wobble the top of the upper case from side to side.

The foot of the Boston turned leg (figure 63) uses the same combination of shapes found on the larger feet in figures 43 and 44, but, as part of creating a tall-reaching form, this foot has a platform below the ball to start an upward thrust. Benno Forman inspected the leg and foot and pronounced them to be particular to Boston in their shaping. He noted, however, that in his experience Boston legs generally have a round tenon that originates from the leg and goes down through the stretcher and the foot to terminate at the floor. In this example, the tenon originates from the foot and goes up into the base of the leg.

The probably New York high chest differs from related Philadelphia work (figure 64) in that the Pennsylvania piece is of solid wood, uses paired pulls on all the drawers—even when they are not of great width—and there is a broad space between the drawers in the stand, as though the middle legs continued up between them. A similar spacing appears on the related English piece. The legs on figures 61, 62, and 64 do, in fact, end in round tenons that are housed into blocks glued behind the skirt boards.

The visual and constructional risks of these tall cases make them part of the best of baroque classicism. A similar attitude toward design is found in the chairs of the period. Like the high chest, they are often crowned by elaborate crests perched on tall, slender forms that lack the solid construction found during seventeenth-century severity.

FIG. 64 High chest of drawers, 1700-1730, Philadelphia, Pennsylvania. American black walnut, Atlantic white cedar, and southern yellow pine. Yale University Art Gallery, Mabel Brady Garvan Collection.

FIG. 65

FIG. 66

FIG. 65 Caned armchair, 1690-1700, London, England. Walnut and cane. The Victoria and Albert Museum.

FIG. 66 Leather armchair, 1700-1725, probably New York, New York. Maple and oak; leather, brass nails. Museum of Fine Arts, Boston, Gift of Mrs. Charles L. Bybee.

The London cane chair (figure 65) is one of the most developed of the type. It is dated 1690 to 1700 for it incorporates two dateable features: The first is the placement of the crest rail. Until about 1700 crest rails were put between back posts with finials. After 1700, on fashionable cane- and related panel-back chairs, the crest rail was placed on top of the posts. (In a third style phase, the back posts and top rail became the one sinuous line now readily associated with the Queen Anne style.) Until about 1700 front legs faced forward; then they raked sideways, as here, and the fronts of the arms also turned outward and provided a welcoming feeling.[2] The surfaces are carved with plunging baroque forms, and areas of the solid wood are pierced to an almost lace-like appearance, but one can still read the parts. For example, the boards flanking and below the cane panel retain their sharp edges. The overly severe, lower edge of the back's bottom board would have been obscured by a fat cushion.

Because of the shaping of the back posts above the seat, the armchair (figure 66) has been assigned both to Boston and to New York.[3] It was perhaps the finest of the surviving examples until it was charred

a few years ago in a fire. The shaping of the front stretcher is echoed in the crest rail, but there the leafage creates an arching form. The turnings are finely drawn; the scrolled front ends of the arms turn outward to welcome the sitter. Many such chairs used prized imported Russian leather for their seats and backs.

Less expensive than leather chairs were banister backs that placed lathe-turned elements over rush seats as in figure 67. A comparison of its finials and back posts with those of the London cane chair (figure 65) shows how readily English details were followed. The spindles in the back were created by turning units similar to those that form the side posts above the seat; these were cut in half with their flat sides usually placed forward—a similar procedure was used to make the applied split spindles on seventeenth-century pieces (figure 41). This banister back is one of the great Massachusetts statements that bespeaks precarious beauty: the tops of the front legs become ever thinner until they become round tenons that stick into the seat lists.

FIG. 67 Banister-back chair, 1700–1725, eastern Massachusetts, possibly Boston. Soft maple and hickory; old black paint grained with red lines. Yale University Art Gallery, Mabel Brady Garvan Collection.

Its surface was painted black and grained with red lines. It is unusual among its type in that the seat pitches forward: the back edge is about an inch higher than the front.

Slat-back chairs, often referred to as ladder backs, were less expensive than the more complex banister backs. The chair in figure 68 has the tall, lean, risky stance of the period. It is typical of the form's development in New England. The sausage-turned front stretchers were quickly made echoes of the more costly spiral-shaped form. The slats increased in height as they moved to an arched top slat—like the arching of the crest rails on the two previous chairs. In the verticals, the size of the ball turning is forceful, and those of the finials sit on slender reel and ring turnings. The dark brown paint features the gold striping that became fashionable early in the nineteenth century; under it is red paint.

Slat-backs became the "workhorse" of the chair form. (From the middle of the eighteenth century, Windsors paralleled them as useful, sturdy seating objects.) Although detailing would change to reflect new styles as they appeared, the slat-back's basic constructional features remained constant. By 1725 in New England, the ball-turned accents, which were features left over from the seventeenth century, became rings; the front stretchers developed a central ring flanked by baluster forms, as had appeared earlier on banister-back chairs. By the end of the century, the rings in the posts became slender accents, and they disappeared altogether on countless nineteenth-century New England expressions of the form (figures 232 and 233).

Similarly, during the eighteenth century, there were thousands of tables made with turned legs connected by stretchers below simple board tops. As on slat-back chairs, their decorative shaping became thinner as the century progressed. Those with bold decorative turnings are usually early (figure 33).

In Philadelphia, and the Delaware River Valley in general, the characteristics of slat-back chairs were very different (figure 69). Using the tall and lean stance of the period, the back posts have tapered feet and decrease in circumference as they mount to fairly standard finials that employ reels, flattened balls, and pointed tops. Their graduated slats are usually serpentined on both edges. The front legs have reel and ball shapes that form balusters below the seat, and the feet use a larger version of the combination. While in New England the front stretchers of slat-backs developed central accents after about 1720, in the Delaware Valley the shaping remained a constant from the beginning. As on figure 69, they have a central ring flanked by reels and balusters, which move to tapered ends. Many chairs from this region, as on this crisply turned example, have thin ring accents in the middle of all the ring and ball shapes. This chair features tiger-grained maple coated with a dark finish. Together they allow the surface to look like figured walnut or mahogany. (The process of darkening maple is discussed in Section 14.)

FIG. 69 Slat-back chair, 1750–1810, Delaware River Valley. Soft maple, including tiger maple; stained dark; early rush seat. Yale University Art Gallery, Mabel Brady Garvan Collection.

American Freedom

The greater freedom to open up designs is one of the factors dividing American forms from English work. Long before Frank Lloyd Wright cantilevered the Edgar J. Kaufmann house, Fallingwater, over a stream, American furniture designers had taken advantage of easily available wide boards to thrust forms into space. England had long been short of local woods, importing wood from various sources, and then from the new American colonies. This meant that in England, tabletops made of local woods usually employed several pieces and rarely projected far beyond their supporting frame. The tables in this section rake their legs dramatically and thrust out their tops.

Most early English and American drop-leaf tables have vertical legs, and when the leaves are open they are supported by gates made of posts and rails. Their turnings usually match those on the legs and stretchers, and when opened they keep the table from tipping sideways. Some American drop-leaf tables used swinging brackets instead of gates (figure 70). These were fixed below into the side stretchers. Because of the shape of the brackets, collectors have called these butterfly tables. Without gates to stabilize the form when opened, the feet were given a wide stance by raking the legs outwards. This construction was less expensive than using gates while providing less-interrupted knee space.

Most tables using swinging brackets are small in scale; the table in figure 70 is rare in its large size, the massiveness of its turnings, the presence of original feet, and the retention of much of its first coat of paint. It is visually exciting because of the power and scale of the thrusting legs, which play against the outward flow of the brackets and the projecting leaves.

Small tables with turned legs are often termed "tavern tables," although the form was widely used. Both English and American collectors have long prized the type because of their usefulness in modern homes. Consequently, the form has been the joy of fakers in both countries. Tripod tables were customary in England, perhaps because three legs took less wood and labor, and they do not wobble on uneven floors. The form is relatively rare in America. The shape

FIG. 70 Drop-leaf table, 1700–1730, West Newbury, Massachusetts, area; according to tradition, it came from the Lydia Poore house in West Newbury. Maple; original brown paint. Museum of Art, Rhode Island School of Design, Furniture Exchange Fund.

FIG. 71

FIG. 73

FIG. 72

FIG. 74   FIG. 75

of the turnings of figure 71 suggests a Pennsylvania origin. Its magic lies in the shaping and movement of the parts and their dry, untouched surface that retains much of its original red paint.

Tables 72 to 75 are from the Portsmouth area of New Hampshire, and placed together they allow the eye to play and choose. Most have Spanish feet that slip the eye up from the floor to the slender, artfully drawn double-baluster turned legs to the line of the skirt rails. Two have ring turnings just above the feet. On figures 72 to 74, the skirts drop in the center and echo the outline of the legs. The skirt of figure 75 has shaping that rises in the center and opens up the form. When objects reach this level of artistic achievement, it is the particular eye of the viewer that must decide which example is most pleasing. Figure 72 has much of its original coat of red paint, but long ago the base was given a coat of dark green that has gained considerable patina. Early dealers and collectors often repainted a base, to clean it up and make the form dramatic, while not recoating the top so it could retain the much loved "scrubbed top" look.

A comparison of these four oval-top tables with that in figure 33 shows it to be a link between seventeenth-century forms and the early rural work of the next century. Figure 33 has an early rectilinear stance, the weight and quality of turned parts found on the butterfly table, and a degree of play in its use of an oval top, but it has not gained the freedom provided by slender raking legs.

FIG. 71 Circular-top table, 1710–50, probably Pennsylvania. Maple and pine; original red paint. Museum of Art, Rhode Island School of Design, Furniture Exchange Fund.

FIG. 72 Oval-top table, 1725–40, Portsmouth, New Hampshire, or southern Maine. Maple and pine; original red paint, base covered with later dark green paint. The Metropolitan Museum of Art, gift of Screven Lorillard, 1952 (52.195.4).

FIG. 73 Oval-top table, 1725–40, Portsmouth, New Hampshire, or southern Maine. Maple. Location unknown.

FIG. 74 Oval-top table, 1725–40, Piscataqua River area of New Hampshire and southern Maine. Maple and pine; gray-blue paint under old brown paint. Old York Historical Society, York, Maine.

FIG. 75 Oval-top table, 1725–40, Piscataqua River area of New Hampshire and southern Maine. Maple; originally painted red; some light bluish-green drippings; later coats of paint removed and a muddy varnish applied. Winterthur Museum.

THE QUEEN ANNE STYLE

The English version of the new style developed during the reign of Queen Anne (1702–14) became more robust during the years of George I (1714–27), and gained activity of line during the first years of George II (1727–60). In America, the term Queen Anne is used for all of this early cabriole leg material, although some divisions will be made here to facilitate looking. The Queen Anne fashion appeared in Boston about 1725, at first with turned feet, and after about 1733 claw-and-ball feet became a more expensive option: chairs with "New fashioned round seats" (figure 91) were first recorded in Boston in 1729. A couch with "horsebone feet" (cabriole legs) was sold there in 1730. In 1732, "6 Leath[er] Chairs maple frames hosbone round feet [cabriole legs with turned feet] & Cus[hio]n Seats" were recorded. In the same year, "8 Leathr Chairs horsebone feet & banist[er] backs" (banister-shaped splats) were purchased. In 1733, chairs with claw (and ball) feet were recorded.[1] The style may have arrived later in Philadelphia, for the first mention yet known there was in 1739: "1/2 Duz: Crookt foot Chairs & Arm D[itt]o" (cabriole leg side and arm chairs).[2] Further research may find an earlier recorded date. Baroque classicism continued to affect casework: strict containment in tall pieces topped with pediments; pilasters or columns placed either side of rectilinear masses filled with drawers (figure 111) or faced with paneled doors. This architectural styling for the upper half of a large piece would continue in the rococo period. More intimate forms such as tables, chairs, dressing tables, and the lower half of high chests of drawers combined the baroque's boldness with quiet Chinese forms that played wood against the spaces left as voids.

Scholars' rocks (figure 76) reflect the Chinese taste for visual play between mass and space. At the earliest dates, they were part of a garden setting where, like Chinese landscape paintings, they represented a microcosm of the world, and their worn, open forms served as instigators of contemplation. During the Sung dynasty (960–1279), scholars brought them into their studies where some functioned as brush rests, ink stones, or seals, but mostly they were larger and enjoyed for their provocative shapes. The contemplative forms were depicted in paintings and prints. As with the scholars' rocks, the delineated spaces were as important as the wood in early Chinese furniture (figures 77 and 79).

FIG. 76 Print showing a scholars' rock, related to images from *Mustard Seed Garden*, edited by Li Yü, vol. 1, 1679; vols. 2 and 3, 1701; vol. 4, 1818. Polychrome woodblock printing on rice paper. Richard Brown Collection.

Early Chinese chairs varied as to how they treated the visual unity of the top rail and back styles. Some integrated the vertical and the horizontal line so there was a flowing union. This became the look associated with the Queen Anne style. Others, as in figure 77, projected the top line outward, and this instigated the ears on Chippendale-style chairs. The early eighteenth-century London chair (figure 78) carries its dependence

FIG. 77

FIG. 78

FIG. 77 Chair, 1650-75, China. Huanghuali.
The Minneapolis Institute of Arts.

FIG. 78 Chair, 1710-20, London, England.
Woods unknown; japanned. Location
unknown.

FIG. 80

on Asia to the extent of finishing it to a decorated lacquer look. During the second quarter of the eighteenth century, Boston produced a few chairs with straight-edge serpentine-shaped splats and back stiles rounded above the seat. The Chinese stand (figure 79) has the cabriole legs, paired reverse-curve skirt shaping, and sense of open quietness that inspired Queen Anne–style lines and spaces. This attitude moved into Japan to create such delicately drawn forms as the table in figure 80. In England and Ireland (figure 81), such forms took on a firmness that made its way to the colonies; in 1713–14, for example, Boston imported one hundred English tea tables at the cost of £13.10s.[3]

FIG. 79 *Xiangji* (incense stand), seventeenth century, China. Huanghuali. Courtesy, Christie's, New York.

FIG. 80 Center table, 1670–90, Japan. Wood unknown; lacquer and engraved mother-of-pearl. Courtesy, Mallett and Son, London.

FIG. 81 Tea table, 1740-70, Ireland. Mahogany
and pine. The Victoria and Albert Museum photo
archive; David Stockwell photograph.

Besotted by the Beauty
of a Queen Anne Leg

Not everyone in the American furniture field approves of my schol-arly emphasis on aesthetic issues. In the early 1980s, a disgruntled colleague warned a symposium audience about "those who are besot-ted by the beauty of a Queen Anne leg"—as he sought to protect the audience from my concern with beauty as a major factor in why an object was made and may be valued today. The time was at the begin-ning of the "material culture" approach to objects that can value the cultural role of a piece over any aesthetic concerns. The most ex-treme version of this attitude dismisses all high-style objects as irrel-evant to material culture studies, for they represent such a tiny part of what was present in households. I prefer to include all materials of a given time, recognizing that expensive things, whether urban or rural, were appreciated by many and that their look conditioned the appearance of even simple things made with some pretension to fashion.[1]

The offhand remarks about being besotted by beauty helped me see my own philosophy more clearly, and during my evening talk I embraced my colleague's besotted sentence as an important way of both understanding and enjoying earlier furniture. Outside tightly constricted communities, buyers were free to select from a variety of makers who produced similarly priced products. One person could influence the production of rural shops and the buying habits of lo-cal households, as when the style of a group of Hadley chests made in the Springfield area of Massachusetts was conditioned by a patron to whom many living in the area were indebted.[2] But most households, both urban and rural, chose on both aesthetic and monetary grounds from a variety of shops.

This section provides an opportunity to compare an array of Queen Anne–style forms, and their legs, from different areas and economic levels. I could have added many aesthetically poor objects in each category but prefer to discuss aesthetic achievements.

Many Americans hold, chauvinistically, that early American works are necessarily better than their European counterparts, and cite as proof that Americans understood line while the English did

FIG. 82 Cabinet-on-stand, 1710-25, London, England. Walnut, oak, walnut veneer, and ash cross banding. The Victoria and Albert Museum.

not. To counter this oversimplified attitude, I have provided the
English cabinet-on-stand (figure 82) that uses the quiet Chinese
containment of forms to calm the baroque passion for movement.
The London cupboard superbly harnesses the majesty of boldly
formed legs, and the cupboard has tightly drawn, beautifully formed
edges: the corner chamfering starts on the stand as a broad "lamb's
tongue"; it then moves quietly up the corner of the case, increasing
as it mounts the cornice. Where this piece differs from American
work is in enriching all the surfaces—including the legs—with patterned veneers. The understated line and enrichment made this
piece appropriate for a wealthy, culturally sophisticated setting.

Like the forms of the ceramics that would have been used on it,
the original concept of the London rectangular-top tea table (figure
83) came from China. The legs, skirt rails, and tray-like top are
discernible as separate areas but join in quiet unity. Some English
rectangular-top tea tables had silver trays that lifted off, and possibly
a few American tables followed this precedent.[3] At least one Philadelphia tea table has a sheet-iron top that was painted white with gilt
decoration.[4] The skirt rails of the Virginia table (figure 84), with a
long convex profile that moves gently into the curve of the knees, are
slightly interrupted by a recess at their centers. In profile (right front

FIG. 84 Tea table, 1740-50, Williamsburg, Virginia. Mahogany, black walnut, oak, and yellow pine; most of one leg, molding on top, and parts of the rails replaced. Colonial Williamsburg Foundation.

and back left), the legs remain, like those on the English piece, much the same dimension from the skirt rails to the end of the carved rather than lathe-turned feet. Seen from the other angle (front left and back right), the spreading form of the feet relates them to the Anglo-American lathe-turned feet as found on figure 85. Although this quiet unity of leg and foot is rare in American furniture, a Boston japanned high chest of drawers of the same date, and its companion dressing table, benefit from the same Asian-English tradition.[5]

Walnut was the standard fashionable wood for high-style forms during the Queen Anne period, and its rich browns worked well with the style's graceful shapes. Mahogany was occasionally employed during this period, but its often richly patterned grain made it the wood most used for high-style forms during the ensuing Chippendale style. A major exception was Philadelphia, where many cabinetmakers continued to use locally available walnut even for complex objects. If chosen with care, it can show grain patterns as rich as those associated with mahogany.[6]

The use of mahogany for the turned-foot, highly style-conscious tea table (figure 85) suggests a midcentury date.[7] It shows the best of Boston's careful integration of quiet parts: the shaping of the legs and the clean outline of the feet; the convex outward curve of the skirt rails following the outward movement of the knees; the reverse curves of the legs condensed in the shaping of the skirt rails to paired cyma forms on either side of a central drop. The top, with re-entrant

FIG. 85

FIG. 86

corners, looks like a tray. The table is fitted with end boards that slide out to support candles; they are faced with applied moldings. The quiet unity of curved and rounded parts allows this table to represent the best sculptural forms made in Boston.

Makers in the major urban American centers—the Boston-Salem area, Newport, New York, Philadelphia, and Charleston, South Carolina—were aware of European styles and handling of line from newly arriving workers and the constant importation of English and

FIG. 85 Tea table, 1740-60, Boston, Massachusetts. Mahogany and pine. Courtesy, Israel Sack, Inc., New York.

FIG. 86 Tea table, 1740-60, probably Connecticut, descended in the Chandler family of Woodstock, Connecticut, and Worcester, Massachusetts. Cherry and pine. The Connecticut Historical Society, Hartford, Connecticut.

Continental pieces. Some rural makers knew European work and pieces made in urban America because they had worked in urban shops. But simpler skills, less wealth, smaller-scale rooms, and the greater freedom for individual expression provided by distance from European precedence combine to give rural work a special character.

The cherry table (figure 86) has rural energy that makes it different than the Boston example: it was probably made in Connecticut, and the feet have sharp edges, the ankles are slender, the legs sinuous, and the skirt is shaped to an actively moving line. The corners of the tray top are pointed. The candle slides use the full width of the end rails and their moldings are taller. The piece has a forceful presence and visual energy that is distinct from the serenity of the Boston expression.

The mahogany dressing table in figure 87 shows the best of Newport's love of tight rectilinear forms that employ flat surfaces. Pointed carved slipper feet, as found on the Irish table (figure 81), move the eye into cabriole legs that are flat on all four sides. The flatness of their outer surfaces relates to the flatness of the surfaces of the case. The edge of the front skirt moves in large reverse curves to a carved shell that neither projects from nor recedes much into the main surface. The only breaks in the front facade are the three lipped drawers that protrude slightly and their brasses. Lipped drawers that overlap the case act as stops and keep out dust. The molded edge of the top has little projection, which contributes to the containment of form. Some Newport dressing tables have a cove molding tucked between the case and projecting top, which furthers the sense of solid containment, as found on the block-and-shell knee-hole dressing table (figure 188).

Slipper feet are found on many Queen Anne–style Newport pieces and continue there as an inexpensive alternative to the claw and ball feet during the Chippendale style. Many elegant Philadelphia Queen Anne pieces use a slightly thicker and broader form of the slipper foot, and the shape appears on English as well as Irish pieces.

The legs of the Newport dressing table are not one piece from the floor to the top but employ a constructional practice found on many Newport pieces, a few related Connecticut-made objects,

FIG. 87 Dressing table, 1750-70, Newport, Rhode Island. Mahogany. Courtesy, Israel Sack, Inc., New York.

FIG. 88 Leg from a dressing table, 1750-70, Newport, Rhode Island. Mahogany. Courtesy, Nathan Liverant and Son, Colchester, Connecticut.

and some English work. The case is built like a box: the front and sides are dovetailed together. Where the legs meet the case they are reduced in size—the outer faces are cut away (figure 88), and the remaining four to six inches extend inside the case. The extension was glued into the corner and supported there by glue blocks. This construction has become known as "detachable legs," as though one bought the object and assembled it at home, which was not the practice. (All of the pieces with this form of construction that were exported to the South use northern woods for the glue blocks that secure the legs in place.)

Newport's love of forms with a tight skin produced two basic expressions during the Chippendale period that were drastically different in cost. The first, like the dressing table, is easily recognized again on the high chest of drawers in figure 163. The second expression pulsates with blocking and shells (figure 155). In both, the action is one of containment that uses smooth surfaces.

Many collectors, even those with a modest budget, who choose to purchase American works seek out the finest urban statements they can afford, seeing them as among America's greatest artistic achievements. In price, great rural forms have lagged far behind even weak urban work, for, to many, they seem to be on the fringe of America's best furniture. That situation was slightly adjusted when, in 1997, the Connecticut dressing table in figure 89, which had been estimated at $50,000 to $80,000, brought at auction $387,500 because of its form and condition.

The skirt rail has longer reverse curves than on the Newport example, and it activates the center by recessing small, paired reverse curves below a shell placed within a drawer; together the shell and the recess form a niche. Part of the excitement of this piece is how the active line of the top plays against the vertical shaping of the skirt and the outward curves of the knees. The movement of the legs is more like that of the Connecticut than the Boston tea table.

About thirty pieces with shaped tops are known by makers from the Wethersfield area of Connecticut and the Hartford, Deerfield, and Northampton regions of Massachusetts. Since the form is greatly desired by collectors, some pieces that started with rectangular tops now have shaped tops.

The dressing table in figure 90 is like a creature walking slowly, first one foot and then the other, into our presence. I have used an early photograph of it in "as found condition." Since this picture was taken, new double half-round moldings have been applied where they were missing around the drawers. It once had turned drops fixed into the small straight lines of the skirt. I have shown it "in the rough" to raise the question proposed during the discussion of early surfaces in Section 3: would you have altered the surface by putting back the moldings? The areas they once covered had achieved age

FIG. 89

FIG. 90

quality. Replacing the moldings does restore some of the maker's intended configuration, but when found the piece had a warm, consistent patina. (The drops are still missing.)

It is made of maple and uses black lines on a red ground to suggest a patterned wood, perhaps a veneered surface. There are a group of high chests of drawers with similarly shaped legs and feet that carry dates in the 1730s, and they are associated with the Windsor area of Connecticut. They are painted black and use yellow

FIG. 89 Dressing table, 1740-70, Connecticut (see text). Cherry and pine. Courtesy, Sotheby's, New York.

FIG. 90 Dressing table, 1730-40, Windsor, Connecticut, area. Maple; black graining on red paint. Early photograph from the author's files.

FIG. 91 Chair, 1730-55, Boston, Massachusetts. American black walnut and soft maple; seat covering not original. Yale University Art Gallery, Mabel Brady Garvan Collection.

paint to depict fanciful animals and floral life in imitation of elegantly japanned Boston pieces.[8]

This, then, is one of several very personal emulations of a sophisticated Boston taste. In the dressing table, the maker has integrated large turned feet, straight ankles, and thundering knees—which relate in scale to the feet—and the more than half-circle cutout in the skirt. That central opening helps keep the case from having a boxy appearance. Such pieces may be approached as folk or plain-style paintings that are about line and a balance of parts, as will be discussed in Section 28, under figure 226.

Early Queen Anne chairs continued the straight seat edges as found on William and Mary chairs, but as the style evolved they soon gave way to the more expensive curving seat rails that echo the movement of the front legs and back. As on the Massachusetts example (figure 91), the front legs went from the floor to the top of the seat rail, and the front and side seat rails tenoned into them (figures 91 and 92). The area where they meet is about two-and-

FIG. 92 Detail from figure 91.

three-quarter-inches high. If this height had been continued from leg to leg, the mass of the rail would have been visually too thick for the rest of the design, and thus the center part of the lower edge was cut away to lighten the line. The inner part of the top of the front legs and the inside edges of the front and side seat rails were cut away to leave a lip that keeps the loose upholstered seat in place (figure 92). The front seat rail in that image has four notches indicating the chair was number four of the set; the slip seat had a corresponding set of notches so the seat and chair could remain together. (Despite this careful numbering, the seats within a set rarely remain in their original chair.) Since chairs receive more motion abuse than other furniture forms, many have stretchers that connect and stabilize the legs. The lathe-turned stretchers developed during the William and Mary period continued to be employed in many American centers throughout the Queen Anne period even though their straightness does not work well with the objects' curvilinear movement. Despite the slight discord of turned stretchers, the Boston chair in figure 91 expresses in a Boston way the quiet vertical dignity developed in England during the last years of Queen Anne and the first years of George I. In Section 12, we will look at a group of contemporary pieces made in Boston that are more vigorous in attitude.

Philadelphia began the style with quiet early Queen Anne forms but moved quickly to the expressive active line of later George I and early George II. The Irish or London chair (figures 93 and 94) is the kind of merchant-level Anglo-Irish product from which Philadelphia drew inspiration. It does not have great lines, perhaps because it is by a worker who did not have the quality of eye required in

FIG. 93 Armchair, 1740–55, probably Ireland, possibly London. Mahogany. The Victoria and Albert Museum photo archive; David Stockwell photograph.

those who worked for court-level patrons. The best eyes in America could take such pieces and turn them into great forms.

The features that directly relate the Irish-London and Philadelphia chairs (figures 95 and 96) are the sense of breadth, the use of a similar seat construction, trifid feet, shell-carved knees, and movement of arms and their scrolling front ends. A handful of Philadelphia Queen Anne chairs used turned stretchers, but many incorporated flat stretchers. The flat version appears in some New England chairs, but there they are thicker (figure 105).

The Philadelphia armchair in figure 95 plays with space. The outlines of the back, arms, and legs enclose it. With counterpointal reverse curves, the lines move you around the form: up from the feet to the seat rail, around the seat rail to the back stiles, and up and around the splat, which is a play of related forms. The greater mass of the splat is in the upper half; the crest rail is topped by a simple crowning line. Viewed from

FIG. 94 Same as figure 93.

FIG. 95

FIG. 96

the side, the splat is seen to have a reverse curve, with the lower part pushing forward to support the lumbar curve of the sitter. Many Philadelphia Queen Anne chair splats are veneered, but it is very unusual, as here, to also use veneer on the seat rails. The inner curves of the back stiles (between the arms and seat) are separate pieces of wood glued onto the basic stiles that go from foot to top rail.

This and the following chair use a form of seat construction found in 95 percent of Philadelphia Queen Anne and Chippendale chairs: the rear tenons of the side seat rails go all the way through the back stiles and are wedged in place (figure 97). It cost sixpence more to have this construction,[9] but it guaranteed a firm joint. This construction appeared in some chairs made in Yorkshire, England;[10] it is known in a few New York Chippendale chairs,[11] and, during the Queen Anne and Chippendale periods, in Connecticut chairs made under the influence of Philadelphia shop practices (figures 99 and 182). With the advent of neoclassical styling, about 1785, the construction appeared elsewhere, particularly in Rhode Island.

To eliminate the stretchers and thus open the base, and to provide an uninterrupted sweeping line around the seat, such

FIG. 95 Armchair, 1740–55, Philadelphia, Pennsylvania. Walnut and pine. Winterthur Museum.

FIG. 96 Armchair, 1740–55, Philadelphia, Pennsylvania. Walnut. Winterthur Museum.

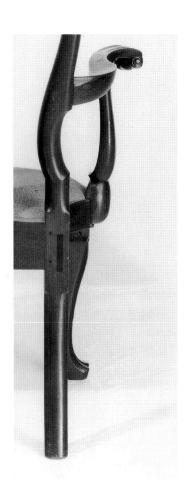

Philadelphia chairs adopted a special English form of seat construction: the front legs do not go from the floor to the top of the seat rail; when they reached the seat they were reduced to round tenons, which came up through the deep rails and were wedged in place from above. The very deep front and side rails are mortise-and-tenoned together over the front legs (figure 98). The new continuous slender front line, that is only two-and-one-eighth-inches high, did not need visual lightening between the legs, and there is no horizontal shaping. Since the rails are so deep from front to back, it would have needed considerable work to reduce the surface to leave a lip to hold the slip seat in place. Therefore, on this form of seat, the containing rim is applied. As a display of beautifully integrated parts, this chair is one of the great pieces of American eighteenth-century sculpture.

The Philadelphia armchair (figure 96) has knee shells flanked by scrolls on the knee brackets. A larger version of the combination crowns the back. The splat and seat rails are not veneered, but money was spent to have the back posts rounded above the seat. The splat, which uses four reverse curves on each side, is less focused on its upper third.

When pieces reach the level of accomplishment found in these two Philadelphia armchairs, deciding between them becomes a matter of personal eye: which works better for the viewer? The first, without rounded stiles, keeps the eye to the plane of the back, and one moves back and forth between it and the shapes below. The rounded stiles allow you to more easily move through the design. Both, as in Chinese scholars' rocks, let the eye play with solids and voids.

The Boston and Philadelphia chairs illustrate their region's best urban high-style work. The side chair (figure 99) exemplifies the finest rural high-style work—the most style-conscious and expensive product of its region. The chair was one of a set owned by Dr. Ezekiel Porter (1707–1775) of Wethersfield, Connecticut. They retain their original flamestitch needlework seat covers. This great Connecticut side chair uses two constructional features associated with Philadelphia that had their origins in England: the deep form of seat rail with an applied containing rim, as in figure 98, and side rails that tenon through the stiles. Both constructional features could have arrived in Connecticut directly from England, but since the first is associated with London, and the second with the northern county of Yorkshire, the most likely source is Philadelphia, where they appeared together. Also Philadelphia-like is the sense of open space contained by wooden parts. Several Connecticut makers worked for a time in Philadelphia before developing as important makers in Connecticut. Looking at the handling of line, the quietness of Massachusetts styling is evident, but the openness of the back and sinuous grace is more like that found in the Philadelphia armchairs. New, and typical of a group of Connecticut pieces, is the lean quality that begins at the front feet and with a feline grace moves up and around a narrow splat. Narrow splats are known in very early European versions of the style,[12] but the slenderness of the baluster form, with a silhouette of a ring at its neck, is probably the maker's invention. A provincial note is seen in the chamfering of the rear legs, and how their bottom few inches angle backwards to keep the chair from tipping over when a sitter leans back. In figure 95, the bottoms of the back legs curve gracefully to provide the deep stance.

FIG. 99 Chair, 1740–60, Wethersfield, Connecticut. Cherry, soft maple, and pine of the *taeda* group; upholstered with its original flamestitch needlework. Yale University Art Gallery, Mabel Brady Garvan Collection.

Most of Connecticut's high-style furniture features cherry, and sometimes the wood was stained dark so it would emulate the color of fashionable walnut or mahogany. Cherry's tightly grained hard quality probably contributed to the smooth, gently rolling surfaces featured on many Connecticut pieces. This quality helps differentiate them from the pieces from which they drew inspiration.

Each shop that sold elaborately high-style forms also made less costly versions, as we will see in Section 16. Some makers specialized in inexpensive, vernacular versions of the fashionable. They cut costs by using inexpensive woods, such as maple, quickly made lathe-turned elements that required only round mortise-and-tenon joints,

flat pieces with little shaping, and rush seats that were sometimes edged with thin boards tacked onto the seat lists around which the rush was wrapped. Probably, when in a home, the rush seats were obscured by a cushion. As in high-style work, elements such as the turned parts or the cabriole legs were often purchased from shops that specialized in these features. The light color of maple was made to fit into the prevailing fashion for walnut, and then mahogany, by coloring it, usually below a coat of varnish. In the 1738–51 ledger of the Philadelphia vernacular chair maker Solomon Fussell, it is recorded that maple chairs were "colourd" or "dyed." Black and brown are the colors most often mentioned, but red is listed twice and orange once. Varnishing is mentioned frequently, but usually in connection with older chairs that were in the shop for repairs.[13]

The vernacular Philadelphia armchair (figure 100) has the beauty of the best Philadelphia line made available inexpensively. It mixes turned and simple-shaped parts and has no knee brackets to carry the line of the front legs onto the seat rails.

FIG. 100 Armchair, 1740-55, Philadelphia, Pennsylvania. Maple, rush seat; painted black. Winterthur Museum.

The arms, which continue a simple form developed during the William and Mary period, and the crest rail are sculpted. The rest is turned or sawn from boards. There is, however, a careful attention to line and balance of shapes: the back stiles have a beaded outer edge, and they taper from arm to crest rail. Perhaps the maker's greatest achievement is in the drawing of the lines of the front stretcher, the double reverse curves of the seat rails, the crest rail, and the splat. The latter has an unusually tall straight-sided bottom area. Those straight lines relate to the horizontal lines of the rail supporting the splat, and the top edges of the boards enclosing the seat.

The Boston vernacular armchair (figure 101) lacks the quiet integration of the Philadelphia example, but it has some consistency in its decorative parts: the sculpted front legs have turned feet, and the knee bracket areas are decorated by turnings. (A similar knee decoration is found in England.[14]) The fronts of the back stiles are molded above the seat. The crest rail has simple central carving that angles down toward the splat. The base of the splat has a shaped outline. A similar slight discord of parts is found on the Boston high-style chair (figure 91), where the turned stretchers are not a happy element in a

FIG. 101   FIG. 102

form dedicated to curving elements. Unlike most vernacular chairs, whether urban or rural, the Boston example in figure 101 has a form of seat construction that uses rails of rectangular section that employ squared mortise-and-tenon joints.

Boston exported great quantities of inexpensive chairs, and two elements found on figure 101 may have been the sources for related parts in Philadelphia chairs: the shape of the arms and the turnings on the posts under their front ends. The latter were often made separately from the legs, with their bases turned to round tenons which were housed into holes in the tops of the front legs and secured by pins. The swelling centers and pointed ends of Philadelphia-turned front stretchers may have borrowed their form from the shape of medial stretchers found in such Boston chairs.[15]

Such urban vernacular chairs could have been used in less pretentious areas of major houses or as the best chairs in simpler homes. Rural vernacular chairs, which lack the urban sense of line, were similarly used in a variety of settings. The armchair (figure 102) was less expensive to produce than the preceding two chairs: the front legs are lathe decorated above easily shaped Spanish feet; the side and rear stretchers are not turned; the rush seat is not framed with boards as on figure 100. All of the parts are less elegantly drawn than

FIG. 101 Armchair, 1730-55, Boston, Massachusetts. Maple and oak. Winterthur Museum.

FIG. 102 Armchair, 1730-60, probably coastal New Hampshire or Massachusetts, possibly Boston. Soft maple; rush seat; original brown paint. Dallas Museum of Art, The Faith P. and Charles L. Bybee Collection, Gift of Faith P. Bybee.

on the other two vernacular chairs. This chair is so generic in form it may be from a variety of places influenced by Boston work, possibly the coasts of New Hampshire or Massachusetts. It may also have been a really inexpensive Boston chair by a middling maker. Its interest lies in having a direct presentation of nicely shaped parts, and the retention of its original surface.

The mostly lathe-turned chair (figure 103) continues the vertical and horizontal arrangement developed for banister-back chairs during the William and Mary period. It differs in having a shorter back and a scooped top rail over a baluster-shaped splat that echoes the scooping movement of the more developed Queen Anne crest rail. The configuration of the nicely shaped turnings—finial, back post above the seat, front legs, and stretchers—and the outline of the splat are known on chairs made by the Durand family of Milford, Connecticut.[16] Its nicely worn black paint unites the maple of the turned parts and the pine of the splat and the top and bottom rails of the back.

The red-painted chair (figure 104) is slightly more in-the-latest-fashion in having a top rail that caps the back posts, eliminating the

bilateral feeling created by finials. Once developed, such modest
chairs continued in demand until about 1810. The active shapes of
its turnings and splat, and the retention of feet and original paint,
make it a desirable example of these simple forms. This chair once
had mid to late nineteenth-century black paint with gold striping
surrounding carefully delineated pansies painted on the splat. These
decorative features were accompanied by a patchwork velvet seat covering. The chair could have been left that way and been a choice
example of a charming new use of an early piece. That later work
was so carefully removed the original worn paint remains intact, and
the chair presents itself as it appeared before it was freshened up.
Whether the chair should have been cleaned of later paint seems
unimportant, for either state is informative and neither is so rare as
to make it preferable. Had the original paint not been totally salvage-
able in an undisturbed state, the chair should have been left alone.

FIG. 104 Chair, 1740-1810, New England,
probably Connecticut. Maple and ash, new
splint seat replacing rush; original red
paint (see text). Private collection.

Bold Boston Forms

During the first half of the eighteenth century, Boston was responsible for 40 percent of colonial ships carrying cargo and was the major port of entry for London goods. Many Anglocentric Boston merchants wore English-made clothing and bought English goods, including furniture, for their homes. Boston cabinetmakers sent venture cargo with ship captains to sell in other cities, and Newport, New York, and Philadelphia were major buyers. By 1760 the situation had changed: Newport grew to have about half the population of Boston, and nearly the same number of cabinetmakers. In the 1770s Newport had more vessels than any other colonial town, and it was a major exporter of furniture.[1]

The Boston chair (figure 105) is part of a group that most scholars, including myself, formerly attributed to New York: family histories and a slight crudeness of line made that seem logical. While New York produced great silver in the seventeenth and early eighteenth centuries, its contemporary furniture was less notable. It made some interesting pieces during the Chippendale period, and became a major style center at the end of the century (figures 198 and 215). Recent scholarship has provided a greater understanding of both Boston and New York furniture. As this section shows, the Boston chair drew directly on London styles that in turn borrowed Continental ideas.

There is a group of chairs that are so alike they were until recently thought to be from one set (figures 106 and 107). Close looking divided the group into two sets and gave the first (figure 106) to the Continent, probably Italy, and the other to a London maker who copied the Continental examples (much as Boston borrowed London forms). On both chairs, gilded carving features sea forms: dolphin feet, shells, fish, areas of fish scales, leaf forms, rosettes, and leafage. The probably Italian chair is the bolder of the two: compare, for example, the shell forms on the crest rails. Its back rail and shoe are of one piece of wood; in the London chair they are separate parts.[2] The form of the probably Italian and London chairs was borrowed for the merchant-level London chair (figure 108). It adds a

FIG. 105 Chair, 1730-50, Boston, Massachusetts, carving possibly by John Welch (1711-1789). Walnut, walnut veneer, maple, and white pine. The Metropolitan Museum of Art, Gift of Mr. and Mrs. Benjamin Ginsburg, 1984 (1984.21).

reverse curve to the back stiles above the seat, and veneer enrichment replaces expensive carving on the seat rails and the entire back.

Figure 105 is one of a set of eight chairs that descended from the Boston family of Charles and Grizzell (Eastwick) Apthorp. Tradition states that they were purchased in New York during the 1750s or 1760s and brought by the family to Boston. Now, greater understanding allows them to be seen as part of Boston's handling of chair forms from about 1730 to 1750. The Apthorps owned a rich assortment of furniture including a "Mohogony Cabinet with glass doors," valued at £30, and a "Mohogony Beauro with Glass doors" valued at £32. Either may be the bombé chest of drawers supporting a chest of drawers faced with paired mirrored doors now owned by the Museum of Fine Arts, Boston.

The chair has a powerful presence, if unresolved unity. The stretchers add curving movement to the base, but they conflict with

FIG. 107

FIG. 108

the upward flow of the cabriole legs, and the union of the shaped
stretchers, back legs, rear feet, and turned rear stretcher is clumsy.
The front of the rounded seat is too flat for the curves of the back.
The splat has a visually interesting crotch veneer applied to a maple
backing, but its richness is not recalled elsewhere, except in the
forceful central shell. The leafage flanking the shell seems stunted.
The carving is attributed to John Welch, who worked from 1732 to
1780. During the second half of the century, he produced wonderful carving that included rococo-style frames for portraits by various
artists including John Singleton Copley (figures 110 and 151).[3]

The boldness of the chair sets up a good contrast to Boston's
ability to produce the calmer beauty of figure 91. The Apthorp chairs
also make one of the region's greatest forms more understandable.
Until the reattribution of this group of strong forms, Boston's production of the bombé form later in the century seemed an anomaly.
Such pieces have long been held to be masterful American reinter-
pretations of English designs based on Continental examples. In
1977 the bombé chest of drawers (figure 109) set a record as the
most expensive piece of American furniture sold at auction when
it brought $135,000. Before that only Philadelphia and Newport
pieces had broken the $100,000 barrier.[4] It is a tour de force in

FIG. 107 Chair, 1725-35, London, England.
Walnut; gilt gesso. The Metropolitan
Museum of Art, Bequest of Irwin
Untermyer, 1973 (1974.28.214).

FIG. 108 Chair, 1725-40, London, England.
Wood unknown. The Victoria and Albert
Museum photo archive.

FIG. 109 Chest of drawers, 1780-90, Boston, Massachusetts, possibly from the shop of John Cogswell (1738-1818). Mahogany and white pine. Inscribed in chalk: "Green." The Dietrich American Foundation.

cabinetmaking. Not only do the sides and fronts gently swell as they lift from the base moldings, but the front is serpentined, and the ends of the drawers are shaped to follow the curves of the sides. With the bombé form, it is very important how and where the curving sides transition into the verticals that flank the upper two drawers. Here, the graceful line does not straighten out until it is flanking the top drawer. (On a few bombé pieces, the interior drawer sides follow the curve of the drawer fronts. On this piece, the sides are angled: when the drawers are opened, the fronts project beyond them.) The interior of the case is marked "Green" in chalk, and the piece has been traced back to the wealthy merchant Gardiner Greene. When he ordered this chest of drawers, he specified the most expensive form of brasses available from England: rococo-style, pierced, and fire-gilded units that feature flowers and Chinese motifs.

The visual mass of the bombé chest is related to the bold forms used by John Singleton Copley in his 1764 portrait of Moses Gill (figure 110). The frame, possibly by John Welch, has the same fanci-

ful role as the chest's gilded brasses. Copley could do rococo lightness, as in the portrait of Mrs. Warren (figure 122), but most of his American portraits show a baroque weight that bespeaks an American forthrightness. All the lines and bold areas of color make the eye move to the head, which dominates the upper third of the canvas: the sweeping lines of the blue velvet frock coat and the curving lines of the buttons of the pearl-gray silk waistcoat rush you to the head. The waistcoat is unbuttoned at the throat to feature a white cravat, which is the upper point of three white areas that border the hands and support the head. The coat has London-style closed boot cuffs with embroidered buttons and is lined with gray silk.

FIG. 110 *Portrait of Moses Gill*, by John Singleton Copley (1738-1815). Oil on canvas; frame possibly by John Welch (1711-1789). Boston, Massachusetts. Signed and dated lower left "JS Copley Pinx^{t} 1764." (Frame cropped top and bottom by photographer.) Museum of Art, Rhode Island School of Design, Jesse Metcalf Fund.

Mixing New with Old

The high chest of drawers (figure 111) has been published as a major piece of eastern Massachusetts furniture. Most of it has great aesthetic merit: the fine lines and balanced details of the upper and lower cases are richly enhanced by veneering, inlay, carving, and gilding. It is also an important document, for it was signed and dated in 1739 by Ebenezer Hartshorne of Charlestown, just across the river from Boston, Massachusetts. In 1965 it was the frontispiece of an important book devoted to much of the American furniture collection in the Museum of Fine Arts, Boston. For years I ignored this piece, both when looking at the catalogue and when teaching in the museum's galleries; my eyes just skipped it.

In 1972, the museum created an exhibition of Boston-area furniture to coincide with a conference on Boston furniture, sponsored by the museum and other local institutions. As I entered the galleries at the opening of the show, I was physically confronted by the piece, for it faced the doorway. The prominence of the placement made my mind ask why I had always ignored it, and I decided to stare at the piece until I saw what was really there. It became evident that if one took off the awkwardly shaped legs with clumsy feet and removed the inappropriate finials (figure 112), it really was a great piece. The lower carved, gessoed, and gilded shell is surrounded by lively flame-patterned veneer and brasses. While enclosing the shell, these decorative features established a firm base from which the veneer and brass patterns move up through the upper case to support and flank the upper shell. The arching of the pediment completes the line that begins at the floor and moves up reverse-curve legs and along the edges of the cases. The horizontal action of the upper drawers is halted by the fluted pilasters, which are capped above the cornice by side finials. Areas of the pediment are kept from being too bland for the rest of the facade by star inlays. (Star inlays also enrich the sides of the upper

FIG. 112

FIG. 111 High chest of drawers, 1739, Charlestown, Massachusetts, mostly by Ebenezer Hartshorne (1689-1781). Walnut, walnut veneer, and pine; gilt shells. Legs replaced; finials from Philadelphia; old but not original brasses installed by museum. Inscribed on back of lower case "1739/E. Hartshern." Pencil inscriptions recording repairs in 1808 and 1915. Museum of Fine Arts, Boston, Julia Knight Fox Fund.

FIG. 112 The Ebenezer Hartshorne part of figure 111.

FIG. 113

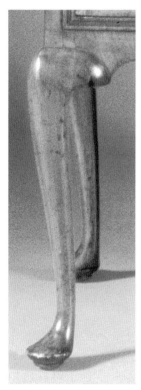

FIG. 114

FIG. 113 Detail from figure 111.

FIG. 114 Detail from figure 117.

and lower cases.) This decorative feature was borrowed from England where at times it appeared, as here, made of small pieces of colored wood, or it was ground into the arched upper glass of a looking glass, or mirrored glass door panels on furniture, to provide a bright accent.

By close analysis it was possible to see that Hartshorne had created a wonderfully integrated whole. But the present legs are awkwardly shaped (figure 113) and the finials are wrong for this piece: Massachusetts finials of this period used tight corkscrew tops on urns, as found on figures 115 and 117. Those on the Hartshorne piece employ only the looser flames found above urns on Philadelphia pieces (figures 116 and 175). (The flames and urns of Philadelphia finials were usually made separately, for the upper part is elaborately carved after being lathe-turned while the lower section is only lathe-turned; thus a replacement using only one part is not surprising.) I could easily understand how parts of the incorrect finials might be on this piece, but the visually disturbing legs presented a more complex problem.

I got on my back under the piece. What I was looking for were joints where the present legs had been spliced onto the corner posts of the lower case in recent years. I found the joints. They are discernible where the inner faces of the legs curve out from the straight lines of the corner posts. (In genuine construction, the leg and the corner post of the lower case are one piece of wood from the floor to the midmolding.) I expected the legs to be wrong because they and the feet are wrong in the line. And I knew such changes happened to early pieces with long legs that had been cut down so that they could be used as storage units in attics or elsewhere.

The changes may have been legitimate repairs, as the pencil inscriptions suggest, or the work of a faker. Fakers who wish to sell a cut-down piece as totally "right" cannot replace the legs from floor to the midmolding, because any knowledgeable buyer will look inside both cases to see whether all the interior woods, including the corner posts of the stand, have proper shrinkage, age color, and wear. Parts that appear only as outside elements can rather easily be altered, for a new finish to the entire exterior of a piece adds legitimacy to the fresh appearance of the added parts. The trick is to leave undisturbed anything that is visible from the inside, where there should be no finish. When the restorer or faker cut off the stumps of these legs, where the line of the corner posts springs out to form the knees, he must have damaged some of the veneer above the cut line, for there are small replacements to the case veneer just above the knees.

I told Albert Sack—a dealer known for his eye who was also at the opening—about the joints, and he got down, looked, and saw. Eventually the base was sent to a hospital to be X-rayed, and the pictures

FIG. 115   FIG. 116

show dowels holding the present legs to the bottom of the corner posts, not an eighteenth-century practice.

When comparing the movement of the new legs to one on the related Boston piece (figure 114), it is easy to see that the top halves of the new legs are too straight. The presence of a knot in the left front leg is also surprising. The new feet are heavy in movement—an early foot shows a quick lower line that curves up from the floor to a sharp edge, from which the upper curve moves quickly back toward the ankle. The new feet are typical of an out-of-the-period turner who has to think about how to do an early turned foot. Not only do the two curves of the feet move ponderously, but also the junction of the two has been made incorrectly soft. Perhaps the restorer or faker hoped to convey a sense of age and wear to this line. We saw the same lack of correct distinctions between parts when we looked at the recently made turned chair in figure 47.

A third feature is incorrect. The original side finials did sit on

FIG. 115 Finial on a high chest of drawers, 1730-50, Boston, Massachusetts, area. Walnut; gilt flame. The Metropolitan Museum of Art, Gift of Mrs. Russell Sage, 1909 (10.125.62).

FIG. 116 Finial on a tall clock, 1765-90, Philadelphia, Pennsylvania. Mahogany. The Metropolitan Museum of Art, Morris K. Jesup Fund, 1948 (48.99).

FIG. 117

these cube-like blocks that extend upward the flatness of the pilasters below them. At the center, however, the cube below the finial is new. It was put there to give the Philadelphia flame the height an urn should supply; it now looks awkward. All three blocks have a thin top board: those at the sides have carefully molded edges, the one at the center a simple half-round edge.

The authoritative power of an illustrated object, particularly when it has graced an important book, was demonstrated by this piece's influence on a collector who owned the related high chest in figure 117. When he purchased it in 1962, its original Massachusetts corkscrew finials were not gilded.[1] Not realizing the Boston Museum's finials were wrong, he had the flames of his beautiful finials covered with gold leaf so they would be as elegant as those on the Museum of Fine Arts's example.

The genuine parts of the Hartshorne high chest are important; therefore, how should the work be used? The museum could discuss what has been changed on its label, and this would follow the growing practice of more informative labels. It could be shown without legs and finials, as one would show parts of an ancient sculpture or an important but cut-down painting. New legs, more accurate in form, could be installed, and copies of appropriate Massachusetts finials made. Alternatively, the piece could be placed in a 1931 period room (the year it was purchased by the museum) to show the colonial revival expectations of that date. Since the museum has many great pieces of the period, I would suggest that the piece be left alone and the informative story given. If it were the major piece in an eastern Massachusetts historical house that intended to represent 1730–50, I would correct the legs and finials, for in such a setting objects should inform viewers about the look of the announced historical time and place.

FIG. 117 High chest of drawers, 1730-50, Boston, Massachusetts, area. Walnut, walnut veneer, and white pine; gilt shells; new gilt on flames of finials. Courtesy, Christie's, New York.

Enriched Surfaces: Imitating Expensive Surfaces and Transforming Awkward Forms

Although maple was a primary wood used for inexpensive New England furniture during the eighteenth century, its blond color was normally either painted or stained until about 1780, when light woods became part of the neoclassical taste for bright surfaces. From about 1720, the figure of tiger maple was exploited to help suggest expensive woods by allowing it to show through a dark finish. The use of patterned maple in effecting an illusion was not a casual decision, for its twisted grain makes it harder to saw and very hard to plane smooth; shallow bites of a very sharp blade are necessary to prevent pulling out bits of the twisted grain.

Solomon Fussell's use of stain on Philadelphia maple chairs in the second quarter of the eighteenth century was noted in Section 11, and the practice was widely employed. The Newport cabinetmaker Job Townsend, Jr. (1726–1778), produced many more stained maple desks (costing about £75) than mahogany desks (priced at about £240).[1] During the walnut period, the color was darker and browner than during the mahogany years. Sometimes the color was achieved by a thin paint (pigment in a binder such as oil, which primarily stayed on the surface). It may have been the final coat, or it may have been covered with a varnish. More normally it was a water- or alcohol-base stain, which penetrated like a dye, finished over with a varnish. Local materials for obtaining the darkening agent included walnut bark, walnut hulls, and butternut hulls.[2] Recipes for coloring stains appear in Robert Dossie's *The Handmaid to the Arts* (London, 1758), a maker's guidebook that was widely owned in America in the eighteenth century. (Thomas Jefferson and Charles Willson Peale had copies.) The 1764 edition includes recipes for many colors, but the relevant ones to this discussion are red, brown, purple brown, dark brown, and a "light red brown . . . it will have greatly the appearance of new mahogany."[3] The New Hampshire cabinetmaker Major John Dunlap (1746–1792) wrote down a recipe "To stain wood to Resemble Mehogany." It includes boiling two pounds of logwood chips (a dark-red heartwood from a tropical tree) in a gallon of water, straining it, and reducing the liquid to one

FIG. 118 High chest of drawers, 1740-70, Salem, Massachusetts. Soft maple and eastern white pine; case colored brown, fans polychromed (see text). Yale University Art Gallery, Mabel Brady Garvan and C. Sanford Bull, B. A. 1893, Collections (by Exchange).

quart. That was brushed onto the maple three times. Then the piece was brushed with a grain-alcohol stain that uses curkmy root (a tropical herb of the ginger family), dragon's blood (a dark-red resinous substance derived from a species of palm tree), and logwood. This was to be varnished.[4]

The high chest of drawers (figure 118) has features associated with Salem, Massachusetts: sharp-edged knees—with that edge stopping abruptly a third of the way down the legs—sharp-edged knee brackets, and a pair of small scrolls at the center of the skirt. The legs and sharp-edged feet are exquisitely shaped. The drawer fronts and moldings use tiger maple. The upper and lower cases, except for the fan-carved drawers, have thin, richly patterned painted graining over the tiger maple, which is slightly visible through the finish to enhance the painted surface. The fan-carved drawers have horizontally painted graining around rainbow-enriched fans.

When a maker did not have the main wood of the case piece in all the necessary thicknesses, he could use two woods and color one to match the other. There are cherry high chests of drawers, for example, that have maple legs which were stained a cherry color.[5] Sometimes only the most intricate or focused-upon part of an object used an expensive wood, and the rest was of a cheaper wood stained to relate. The maple desk with a mahogany desk interior (figure 119) was signed in pencil by the senior Job Townsend (1699/1700–1765). In 1963 the owner asked a dealer to remove the "reddish-brown stain" Townsend had applied to the maple to make it match the mahogany.[6] There are a variety of tiger maple high-style Philadelphia Chippendale pieces—including shell-carved chairs and elaborately enriched high chests—that have been stripped of their darkened surface; they now look naked when placed next to their darker contemporaries.

There is an important caveat when considering the use of a dark finish intended to allow the wood's grain pattern to show: the dark color may be all, or in part, the result of an original or a later varnish that darkened as it aged; the oxidization of an oil that was applied since the piece was made; accumulated dirt; or all of these non-original factors.[7]

Painted graining, especially when it is stylized almost to abstraction, can make an otherwise mediocre piece into a delightful visual experience. The small high chest of drawers (figure 120) has unso-

FIG. 120   FIG. 121

phisticated feet, no knee brackets to join the curve of the legs to those of the skirt, slightly loose-in-line skirt shaping, and small brasses that are not placed according to the traditional habit: on the long drawers they are all placed the same distance from the bottom of the drawers. They would seem to be sinking if they were not part of a dramatic display of colorful, free-moving, painted grain. The maker/decorator has created a major piece of personal art.

The legs on the high chest of drawers (figure 121) are like those found on some tables where knee brackets that join the movement of the legs to that of the skirts are not part of the concept. Rather, the knee seems to move into the corners of the case. The giant curves of the skirt rather clumsily move up to a central dropping curve. The paint turns everything into visual excitement: the case has a red-ochre ground; black curving brushstrokes cover the legs, skirt, and sides; black slashes up the drawers, its action alternating from left to right, and back again to the paint-enriched cornice.

FIG. 120 High chest of drawers, 1735-50, probably southeastern Connecticut. Maple, tulip poplar, and pine; paint grained. New Haven Colony Historical Society.

FIG. 121 High chest of drawers, 1740-65, possibly Maine. Maple and pine. Society for the Preservation of New England Antiquities.

THE ROCOCO PERIOD AND CHIPPENDALE STYLE

FIG. 122 *Portrait of Mrs. James Warren (Mercy Otis)*, ca. 1763, by John Singleton Copley (1738-1815). Oil on canvas. Museum of Fine Arts, Boston, Bequest of Winslow Warren.

Thomas Chippendale was a London furniture maker with a large firm that made items for prestigious clients. In 1754, he produced the design book The Gentleman and Cabinet-Maker's Director. *It was published again in 1755, and a revised, larger version appeared in 1762. Chippendale was not the most famous London maker of his time; William Vile and the firm of William and John Linnell made greater furniture, and designers such as Robert Adam, who worked during the latter years of Chippendale's life, produced more exquisite designs. But when antiquarians and furniture historians began to designate style periods, the name Chippendale was assigned to most of the English rococo-style furniture because of his publication. Chippendale's* Director *shows influences from four styles: Chinese, rococo (which he called French), Gothic, and a classicism that looks both to baroque classicism and to the newer Palladian classicism. Both of these classical stances will be reviewed as part of discussing American classicism at the end of the century.*

Rococo in America

From about 1750 American urban centers expressed their version of Europe's rococo styling that made asymmetrically arranged leaner lines out of baroque's bolder movements. In creating the portrait of Mrs. Mercy Otis Warren (figure 122), the Boston portraitist John Singleton Copley placed the head at the center of the upper half of the canvas, while the body and dress create a triangle that fills the lower right. The counterthrust is in the sloping brown cliff that creates a dark triangle on the left. The hands and flowers give the sitter control over the dark area. A sunlit landscape opens up the upper right edge and pushes Mrs. Warren toward the viewer. She is fashionably dressed in a blue *sacque* dress trimmed with silver braid and rushed silk (bands of dress material gathered and applied) that shimmers in the light. The lace stole and ruffles at her sleeves dance with asymmetrically arranged floral patterns.

The role of a careful relationship of unequal parts is found in an earlier (1746) London design by Henry Copland (figure 123), which shows a cartouche at the right. Its balance is not one of equal sides; rather, as in the scholars' rock (figure 76), it comes from a tension between thrusting and counterthrusting curves. The tea kettle on stand (figure 124) was made in Philadelphia by Joseph Richardson, who probably followed closely one made by the London silversmith Paul de Lamerie in 1744–45 for the Franks family of Philadelphia. The Philadelphia kettle uses an inverted pear shape that narrows to a small foot ring that fits inside the collar of the stand. The stand has cast shell-formed feet and hanging decoration of pierced shells, and animal and vegetable forms. The body of the kettle displays rococo-style enrichment. The handle and legs have reverse curves. Graham Hood has written about the piece: "The richness of the chasing and lightness of the engraving form a counterplay of decorative motifs. . . . This bold, Rococo object is a symphony of sinuous curves and fantastic scrolls in every dimension, of rich and delicate ornament, of mass and void, with an essential, overriding harmony."[1]

The rococo style had only a minor influence on English and American rococo buildings. Like architecture, furniture does not

FIG. 123

FIG. 123 Printed designs from *A New Book of Ornaments*, by Henry Copland, 1746, London, England. Private collection.

FIG. 124 Tea kettle on stand, 1745-55, Philadelphia, Pennsylvania, by Joseph Richardson (1711-1784). Silver and wood. Marked three times "IR" in large rectangle with leaf above. Lower wooden part of handle missing. Yale University Art Gallery, Mabel Brady Garvan Collection.

lend itself to a style devoted to teetering excitement, and most American case pieces continued, in a slightly lighter manner, baroque classicism's careful arrangement of parts. In some regions more than others, these were enhanced by swirling grain behind complexly shaped polished brasses, and carved elements further caught the light. Asymmetry was confined to the patterns of rich wood grain and the lively cartouches placed at the center of pediments of some tall case pieces (figure 175). The forms of chairs opened up to play more fancifully with space: the containment of the Queen Anne style disappeared as raking back stiles joined crest rails at projecting ears, and splats were pierced to complex strap work that allowed light to filter through; playful carved details caused the polished surface to sparkle.

Fig. 124

Urban: Elaborate, Plain, and Vernacular

The early furniture that was made in America resulted from the requirements of the buyers, the abilities of the makers, and the aesthetic and cultural traditions of the region where they worked. In the eighteenth century, buying furniture was a bit like ordering à la carte from a restaurant menu, and rather like making choices when buying a car. The basic furniture form was available without decoration, and the customer could add a variety of "extras." The group of Philadelphia chairs in this section demonstrates some of the looks and corresponding prices possible within the Chippendale chair form in Philadelphia from 1750 to about 1785.

On the eve of the American Revolution, Philadelphia was prosperous and producing exquisite objects. It counted among its most prominent citizens John Cadwalader, who has become better known for his expenditures on furniture and paintings than his military exploits as a general in George Washington's army. The Cadwalader chairs (figure 125) were part of a richly appointed parlor, which included a similarly decorated sofa, easy chair, and pair of card tables. The walls were hung with portraits by Charles Willson Peale in rococo frames. One painting shows John Cadwalader's younger brother Lambert, who stands beside a simplified depiction of one of the chairs. With these furnishings the Cadwaladers were announcing an aristocratic stance. Indeed, the degree of elaboration on the furniture has been recognized as very English in inspiration, and a comparison has been made between the Cadwalader chairs and a design in Thomas Chippendale's *Director* (figure 126). (The Cadwalader chair is not sufficiently close to the Chippendale design for it to have served as a source.)

Much has been written about the side chairs (of which at least eleven were made, for one of the known seven is marked "XI"). Scholars disagree as to their maker, although it is generally thought to have been either Benjamin Randolph or Thomas Affleck. The carver is less certain, and any one of a small group of men seems possible. There is no dispute that these richly ornamented pieces were made in the third quarter of the eighteenth century for the

FIG. 126

FIG. 125 Chair, ca. 1770, Philadelphia, Pennsylvania, possibly by Benjamin Randolph or Thomas Affleck. Mahogany and northern white cedar; manuscript references suggested the color of the new yellow silk upholstery. The Metropolitan Museum of Art, Purchase, Sansbury-Mills and Rogers Funds; Emily C. Chadbourne Gift, Virginia Groomes Gift, in memory of Mary W. Groomes; Mr. and Mrs. Marshall P. Blankarn; John Bierwirth and Robert G. Goelet Gifts; The Sylmaris Collection, Gift of George Coe Graves, by exchange; Mrs. Russell Sage, by exchange; and funds from various donors, 1974 (1974.325).

FIG. 126 Printed design for a chair, from *The Gentleman and Cabinet-Maker's Director*, by Thomas Chippendale, 1754 edition: plate XVI, 1762 edition: plate XV. From reprint of third edition (New York: Dover Publications, 1966).

FIG. 127 Printed design for a chair, from *The Gentleman and Cabinet-Maker's Director,* by Thomas Chippendale, 1754 edition: plate XII; 1762 edition: plate XIII. From reprint of third edition (New York: Dover Publications, 1966).

FIG. 128 Chair, 1755-85, Philadelphia, Pennsylvania. Mahogany and cedar. Winterthur Museum.

FIG. 128

splendid Cadwalader house on Second Street. The features that secure them to Philadelphia are the simple-curved back legs with an ovoid cross section, the use of American white cedar as the secondary wood, and the presence of through tenons (figure 97), which are not found on London chairs. (The splat area is made of three sections: a horizontal-grain piece connects the stiles; vertical-grain parts connect it to the top rail and the shoe.)

The chair is very much a frontal object: the carving of the side seat rails stops abruptly at the stiles and they continue down as plain back legs. The Chippendale design (figure 126) provided for rear cabriole legs that echo the movement found elsewhere. In the eighteenth century such chairs stood against the wall unless they were in use, and that may explain, at least in part, Philadelphia's willingness to leave back legs plain even when the patron paid handsomely to carve the rest of the chair. In October 1999, number "I" from the set sold for $1,432,500 at Christie's, New York, making it at that date the most expensive American side chair.

The Chippendale design (figure 127) was the print source for the Philadelphia chair (figure 128), which is certainly a rare, impor-

FIG. 129   FIG. 130

tant Philadelphia artistic statement that was expensive when it was made and extremely valuable today. It is one of only a few American pieces that use scroll feet. The carver has made his enrichment deeper than is found on English pieces that follow Chippendale's designs. This can be seen as bold American firmness in creating forms, or as the expression of a carver that, when looking at a printed source, overdoes the original intention. The carving is beautiful, but to my eye lacks a spontaneity when handling the material, as though the printed source came between the worker and his creation. Perhaps figure 129 is more exciting as an expression of an enriched form. Although it drew inspiration from English work, its maker created with more spontaneity, and it is more recognizably American. The carver of this elaborate chair seems to have pulled complex shapes out of the wood. Although the back is richly carved, each area has great clarity. The integration of the knee and seat rail enrichment is masterful.

The richly but not ostentatiously finished chair (figure 130) is an example of a beautiful design that borrows basic ideas from England, but in an American manner depends on line rather than ornamentation. The reverse curves of the front legs, crest rail, and splat speak harmoniously; the seat rail shell turns over and increases in size to crown the crest rail; the flutes of the shells are echoed

FIG. 129 Chair, 1755-85, Philadelphia, Pennsylvania. Mahogany and pine. Colonial Williamsburg Foundation.

FIG. 130 Chair, 1755-85, Philadelphia, Pennsylvania. Mahogany and tulip poplar. Yale University Art Gallery, Mabel Brady Garvan Collection.

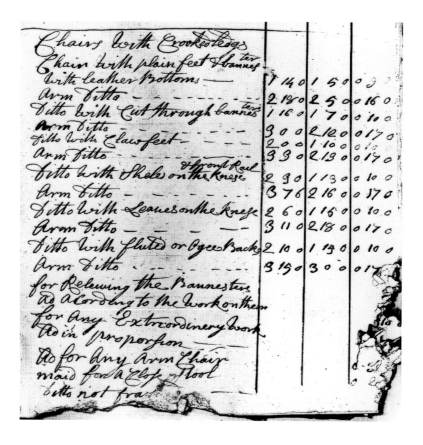

FIG. 131 Detail from the Tyler manuscript, "Prices of Cabinet & Chair ...," by James Hum[?], 1772. Ink on paper. Tyler Arboretum.

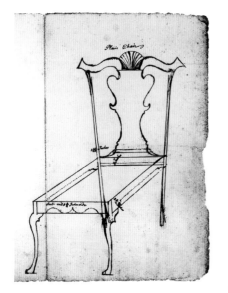

FIG. 132 Detail from a drawing, showing a "Plain Chair," ca. 1766, Philadelphia, Pennsylvania, by Samuel Mickle and/or Jonathan Shoemaker. Ink on paper. Philadelphia Museum of Art, Gift of Walter M. Jeffords.

in the flutes on the back stiles. The chair may have been used in a lesser room in a grand house, but was probably the result of a buyer and maker planning for a principal room in a rich but not ostentatious home.

After the middle of the eighteenth century, there were price lists that could establish the cost of each type of furniture form, both in walnut and in mahogany, and the wages of the journeymen who produced them. These lists were to ensure that the workers in different shops were treated equally. Today, the few price lists that are known help clarify a number of issues, including early terminology for basic forms and individual parts, and when they came into and went out of fashion. The printed version of the 1772 Philadelphia price lists has disappeared, but two manuscript copies are known.[1] Figure 131 shows the listing for cabriole leg chairs. The left column spells out the degrees of complexity of each form. Moving right, the first narrow column gives the price in mahogany, the next in walnut (about a third less), and, finally, at the edge, what the journeyman was to be paid whether he worked in mahogany or walnut. (It is generally assumed that the customer paid the price listed under walnut or mahogany, but the final cost may have been that figure plus the wages of the journeyman.) The chair list was headed "Chairs With Crooked legs," and, just below that, the basic chair was described as "Chair With plain feet & bannester [splat] With leather Bottoms [seats]." It was priced at £1.14s. in mahogany or £1.5s. in walnut.

The configuration of the basic chair, designated "Plain Chair"

FIG. 133

FIG. 134

just above the sketch, can be seen in a drawing of about 1766, figure 132. (It is uncertain who made the drawing, but it is one of a set assigned to the Philadelphia cabinetmaker Jonathan Shoemaker, or his apprentice Samuel Mickle—figures 168 and 169 are part of the group. One of the drawings is inscribed "Samuel Mickle" and dated "1766."[2]) In the chair drawing, the crest rail has a simple central shell and plain ears; the "bannester," or splat, is unpierced; the cabriole front legs end in feet whose profile is similar to that of trifid feet on the plain chair in figure 136. But they may represent the simpler lathe-turned shape of figure 134.

Moving down the list, elaboration and cost increased: "Arm Ditto" was the inexpensive version with arms (figure 135). Next was a chair with "Cut through bannesters": pierced splats. It is followed by the mention of the expensive "Claw [and ball] feet." After the armchair version came a chair with "Sheles on the Knese & front Rail" as on figure 136. More expensive were "Leaves on the Knese" (figure 130). The back posts above the seat could be "fluted" (figure 130) or "Ogee," a molded profile (figure 128). The cost of "Releiving [carving] the Bannesters" was not specified, but was "Acording to the Work on them." After that, the list threw uniformity to the wind,

FIG. 133 Chair, 1730-60, England. Walnut and walnut veneer. The Old Hall, Gainsborough; author's photograph.

FIG. 134 Chair, 1750-85, Philadelphia, Pennsylvania. Walnut and pine. David O. Woodyard Collection; photograph Courtesy Garth's Auctions, Inc., Delaware, Ohio.

FIG. 135

FIG. 136

FIG. 137

FIG. 135 Armchair, 1750-85, Philadelphia, Pennsylvania. American black walnut and pine of the *taeda* group. Yale University Art Gallery, Mabel Brady Garvan Collection.

FIG. 136 Chair, 1750-85, Philadelphia, Pennsylvania. American black walnut and pine of the *taeda* group. Yale University Art Gallery, Mabel Brady Garvan Collection.

FIG. 137 Chair, 1750-85, Philadelphia, Pennsylvania. Walnut. Courtesy, Sotheby's, New York.

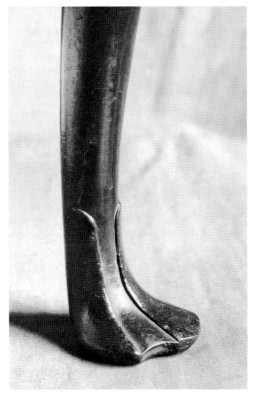

FIG. 138   FIG. 139

stating: "for Any Extreordinery Work Ad in proporsion." Certainly
the Cadwalader chair falls into the "Extreordinery" category.

The plain chair (figure 133) is a parallel English version without
ears. Its back feet are like those on figure 95. The American plain
chairs that follow demonstrate a variety of choices at a rather inexpensive level. They all incorporate a more or less complex shell in
the middle of the crest rail above similar, unpierced splats. Two have
knuckled ears, and the armchair has knuckled ends to the arms. Two
have shells on the knees, and one a shell on the front seat rail. Their
three forms of feet demonstrate increasingly complex and expensive
versions. The simplest is the lathe-turned foot. They are also on
the English chair. The second is the trifid foot that is much easier
to carve while providing the three-prong look and some of the mass
of the expensive and fashionable claw-and-ball form. Figures 138
and 139 contrast a probably Irish and a Philadelphia version of the
trifid foot.

The chairs in figures 136 and 137 provide a particularly helpful
contrast. It is not known if they are from the same shop or if from
two businesses—perhaps they shared the same carving specialist. The
first has trifid feet and plain ears, which made it the cheaper of the
two, but the buyer specified a shell on its front seat rail. The chair
that has the greater mass of boldly carved ears has a greater area of
wood where the splat meets the crest rail. This difference could result from the maker's particular habit of design, or it could be an
adjustment of that area to echo the greater mass of the ears.

FIG. 138 Detail from a stool, 1740-80,
probably Irish, possibly English. Wood
unknown. Robert Wemyss Symonds
Collection of Photographs, Winterthur
Library; Joseph Downs Collection of
Manuscripts and Printed Ephemera.

FIG. 139 Detail from a chair, 1740-55,
Philadelphia, Pennsylvania. Walnut
and pine. Museum of Art, Rhode Island
School of Design.

FIG. 140 Armchair, 1750-85, Philadelphia, Pennsylvania. Maple; stained dark; rush seat. Winterthur Museum.

Today, unless plain chairs have arms that make them both rare and useful, they are generally not given much attention. Many were made by the same eyes and hands that produced the more elaborate designs, and are thus capable of possessing great beauty. The chair in figure 136 is one of the best of the Philadelphia plain chairs. The inward movement of its trifid feet rises to the knee shells, which are echoed on the front seat rail. The back stiles, with just molded outer edges, curve to beautifully shaped, backwardly scrolling plain ears on either side of a complex shell that crowns a nicely integrated splat with counterpointal reverse curves. The lines from inside the large scrolls move up to the lower edge of the crest rail and out to the ears. The bowed back presents the design to the viewer, and from its curve the sitter receives some support.

While the plain chairs provided a less expensive expression of the high-style form, cheaper, partly lathe-turned chairs with rush seats remained available (figure 140). Such chairs were made of maple and often employed figured maple, at least for the splat, so the grain

FIG. 141 Armchair, 1740-90, Philadelphia, Pennsylvania. Maple, including tiger maple; stained dark; rush seat. Courtesy, Israel Sack, Inc., New York.

pattern could show through a thin brown-colored finish. Since the seat construction is not very sturdy, front, side, and rear stretchers were necessary. This example was produced by a chair maker with an extraordinary sense of rhythm and balance, for he achieved a significant sculptural presence. There is a grand interplay of curves and straight edges: the elegant curves of the front stretcher are echoed in the shaping of the seat rails, and the movement is intensified in the shaping of the crest rail. These curves work against the straight lines that include the top edge of the seat rails, and the vertical thrust of the lower part of the splat. The slat-back armchair (figure 141) has plainer feet and boards around the rush seat that work in harmony with the simpler but beautifully drawn parts. It has tiger maple back posts and front seat rail under a dark finish. (A similar chair, but without arms or cabriole legs, appears as figure 69.)

We do not know if any of these plain or vernacular rush-seated chairs were used in a secondary room of a great house or served in the main room of a simpler home.

Regional Differences: Massachusetts and Philadelphia Chairs

Since the end of the 1960s, scholars have made intensive studies of the regional differences in American furniture. This section delineates the kind of physical and visual evidence used to assign a piece to a town or area.

The visual taste seen in the previous section was particular to the Philadelphia region. Sources for the basic forms and details, including constructional features, can be found in England or Ireland, but nearly always the power of Philadelphia's design attitude makes it possible to discern by close looking what is from Philadelphia and what is from the British Isles. In the rare cases where this is an issue, a microscopic analysis of the locally grown woods used for interior construction may determine the origin.

The Massachusetts, probably Boston, chair (figure 142) has a tense leanness in its allover stance and in the execution of its parts—qualities that can be read as Massachusetts characteristics. Nonetheless, nearly the entire look of the chair was borrowed directly from England as seen in figure 143. It was made in London for the Løvenborg Manor House in Denmark in the middle of the eighteenth century. It differs from the American chair in having molded back posts, slightly looser knee carving, and no stretchers. The Massachusetts chair is radically different from the contemporary Philadelphia chair seen as figure 130. The Philadelphia chair uses deep mortise-and-tenon joints between the seat rails (which are four inches high at that point) and front legs. The chair relieves the seat mass by cutting it away between the knee brackets and the central shell, which was carved separately and glued onto the shaped rail. Massachusetts chairs use thin rails of about two-and-a-half inches all the way around the seat.

To compensate for the thinness of the joints between the front legs and seat rails, most Massachusetts Chippendale chairs continued the form of turned stretchers developed during the William and

FIG. 143

FIG. 142 Chair, 1750–85, Massachusetts. Mahogany, white pine, and maple. Yale University Art Gallery, Mabel Brady Garvan Collection.

FIG. 143 Chair, 1745–60, London, England. Mahogany. Courtesy, Brunn Rosmussen, Copenhagen.

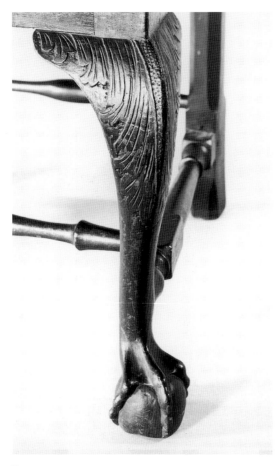

FIG. 144

FIG. 145

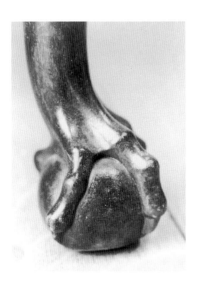

FIG. 146 Detail from a chair, 1750–80, London, England. Mahogany. Mr. and Mrs. Robert W. Chambers, on loan to the Sterling and Francine Clark Art Institute.

Mary period. The back legs of the Philadelphia chair are rounded. Those on the Massachusetts chair are chamfered above and below the stretchers.

The knees of the Massachusetts piece are arrised, or sharp-edged, carrying down the sharp corners of the seat rails. The knee carving is thin and begins at the seat rail (figure 144). On Philadelphia pieces, lush leafage flows around and down from the scroll of the knee brackets (figure 145).

The front feet of the Massachusetts chair (figure 144) are carved in a manner associated with eastern Massachusetts: the knuckles of the three toes are close together, and the side claws rake backward. As with almost all American details and motifs, such features derive from European models,[1] and this form of foot was developed in England (figure 146). On late Queen Anne and Chippendale-style chairs, Philadelphia used trifid feet as quickly carved three-part alternatives to the claw-and-ball form. In eastern Massachusetts, the cheaper alternative was a thicker version of the turned foot found on most of its Queen Anne–style pieces: its greater mass echoed that of the claw-and-ball foot. The chairs in figures 147 and 148 vary only in the cost of their front feet.

The ears on the Massachusetts chair in figure 149 have simple molded faces, and the central shell is a brief, stylized form. These

FIG. 147

FIG. 148

FIG. 147 Chair, 1750–85, Boston, Massachusetts, area. Mahogany. Museum of Fine Arts, Boston, Gift of Mrs. F. Carrington Weems.

FIG. 148 Chair, 1750–85, Boston, Massachusetts, area. Mahogany. Museum of Fine Arts, Boston, Gift of Mr. and Mrs. Henry Herbert Edes.

FIG. 149

FIG. 150

FIG. 151

FIG. 149 Detail from chair in figure 142.

FIG. 150 Detail from chair in figure 130.

FIG. 151 *Portrait of Isaac Smith,* 1769, by John Singleton Copley (1738-1815). Oil on canvas. Frame possibly by John Welch (1711-1789). Yale University Art Gallery, Gift of Maitland Fuller Griggs, B.A. 1869, LHD 1938.

features on the Philadelphia chair are rounded, fuller forms (figure 150). The Massachusetts ears are so typical of that area it is possible to recognize them in contemporary paintings. The Boston portraitist John Singleton Copley did at times borrow details for his sitters—including clothing and furniture and even trees—from prints depicting English portraits, but when he showed American objects they were accurate in detail. For example, his depictions of upholstered easy chairs give evidence of just how the textile was fitted to the chair, including where the strips of textile were seamed. It is easy to see that Copley placed the Boston merchant Isaac Smith in a Boston-area chair (figure 151).

In Philadelphia, the strap work of the splat flows freely from the shoe to the crest rail (figures 130 and 150): three straps move up to become two that end in scrolls; two side straps curve down from the crest rail to end in scrolls on either side of the two overlapping central straps; the splat is bowed to present the design and provide some comfort. (Such chairs are not as comfortable as when splats had a Queen Anne reverse-curve profile, but the bowing of the splat during the Chippendale period provided a better display of the strapwork.) On the Massachusetts chair (figures 142 and 149), four straps move upward from the shoe to visually stop under scrolling that drops from above. The inner straps tightly curl in toward each other. In profile, the splat is straight.

FIG. 152

FIG. 153

The inside of squared, or trapezoidal-shaped, seats usually had corner blocks to strengthen the construction. Massachusetts normally employed a one-piece triangular hardwood block in all four corners, and they were attached with glue and nails (figure 152). Squared-seat Philadelphia chairs used quarter-round softwood blocks with the grain placed vertically (figure 153). In the front, Philadelphia's block was made of two parts that fit around the top of the front leg. At the back, a thin piece was usually placed on the back rail to fill in the space between the rail and the front of the back stile. Then, a quarter-round vertical grain block was glued in place. Both forms of blocks appear in some English chairs: the Philadelphia version being used in the front, and the triangular block in the back. During the Chippendale period, Philadelphia continued to use through tenons (figure 97).

FIG. 152 Detail from a chair, 1750-85, Boston, Massachusetts. Mahogany and maple. Museum of Art, Rhode Island School of Design.

FIG. 153 Detail from a chair, 1750-85, Philadelphia, Pennsylvania. Walnut and tulip poplar. Museum of Art, Rhode Island School of Design.

Urban and Rural Case Pieces: Elaborate and Plain

Section 16 dealt with both complex and simpler chairs made in Philadelphia. Here I address elaborate and plain case pieces made in urban Newport and Philadelphia, and then look at Connecticut's use of Newport ideas to begin the discussion of the flow of ideas from an urban center into the countryside. The Newport desk and bookcase (figures 155, 156, and frontispiece) is a great American achievement. It was made for the Providence, Rhode Island, merchant John Brown and possibly first used in the ostentatious brick house he began to build in 1786. He filled his home with Newport and Philadelphia furniture; his coach came from Philadelphia; his silver from France, England, and various American-style centers. He bought six life-size marble busts from Paris and placed them in pairs at his gateway, in the front hall, and at one end of the parlor. John Brown papered his principal rooms with French neoclassical wallpaper, and this desk and bookcase probably stood in his study against the brightest of them, which features a vivid blue ground (figure 154). The John Brown piece is now at Yale University, and in its stead stands the nine-shell version made for his brother Joseph, which we will look at shortly.

The John Brown desk and bookcase (figure 155) was carefully laid out. The lower case is basically a square: $41\frac{7}{16}$ inches high and $41\frac{9}{16}$ inches wide. Its vertical division uses a three-to-four-part relationship: it is $30\frac{1}{2}$ inches from the floor to the lower edge of the desk lid—three units of about 10 inches—while the full height from floor to midmolding is four units of about 10 inches. Other proportional relationships appear in the bookcase section. The front facade is organized to three verticals by baroque blocking recessed at the center and projecting at the sides.

At the bottom of the piece, the outer edges of the blocking move down through the base molding and on to the bracket feet to end in scrolls. The rectangles created by the verticals of the blocking and the top edges of the drawers are marked with brasses. The drawers are surrounded by cock beading applied to the case. The brasses lead our eyes up to the desk's lid: the side shells and the blocks below

FIG. 154 First-floor southwest room of the John Brown House, Providence, Rhode Island, 1786-88. Originally, a doorway, where the desk and bookcase now stands, led into a side hall that gave access to an outside door. The wallpaper is a copy of the original French paper. The nine-shell desk and bookcase belonged to John's brother Joseph (seen also as figure 157). Figure 155 probably originally stood in this room. The roundabout chair is seen again in figure 162. Paintings of such interiors show chandeliers without candles unless they are lit.[1] The Rhode Island Historical Society.

FIG. 155   FIG. 156

them were made separately and the four pieces applied to the lid. (Only the recessed shells of the lid and central door were carved from the solid.) Above, narrower blocking rises to smaller shells. The pediment's two blocked panels pull the eye toward the central, fluted plinth. The short, tight corkscrew finials are typical of Newport. Rosettes mark the beginnings of the cornice moldings that move down to support side finials on plain plinths; these cap the engaged fluted quarter columns below.

Many German mahogany pieces that are similar to that in the print (figure 161) frame light-colored mahogany drawer fronts, desk lid, and pediment board with ebony moldings.[2] To contain and outline the tall, light-colored Newport desk and bookcase, the upper case is framed by dark mahogany: the cornice moldings, the moldings on the circular cutouts on either side of the central plinth, the three finials, and the quarter columns. The related six-shell desk and bookcase at the Metropolitan Museum of Art, New York, has dark top moldings and finials.[3] On occasion, American high-style pieces used black paint or a scorched surface to provide a dark frame.[4]

The sliding shelf above the long drawers has two brass button pulls that were placed to relate to the side hinges, rather than put over the drawer brasses. To serve properly, the hinges had to be that

FIG. 155 Desk and bookcase, 1760-90, Newport, Rhode Island, probably by one of the Townsend-Goddard families (also see frontispiece). Light and dark mahogany, American black cherry, chestnut, and eastern white pine. Yale University Art Gallery, Mabel Brady Garvan Collection.

FIG. 156 Interior view of figure 155.

FIG. 157 Desk and bookcase, 1775-85,
Providence, Rhode Island. Mahogany
and white pine. The Rhode Island
Historical Society.

far out; putting the pulls under them keeps the hinges from being
isolated, bright accents that would pull the eye away from the upward
movement of the blocking and drawer brasses.

The center and right part of the bookcase doors are hinged
together (figure 156) and open in an accordion fashion. Inside,
there are grooves in the upper two-thirds of the vertical boards for
adjustable bookshelves. Each American-style center had basic ways of
handling the interior of the desk section, and this one is typical of
Newport's manner. The faces of the small drawers over the pigeon-
holes are shaped to recessed niches.

The John Brown example is one of nine Newport block-and-
shell desk and bookcases with six shells. A nine-shell piece made for
John Brown's brother Joseph (figures 154 and 157) has four rather
than the normal three drawers in the base, so the extra one can carry
an additional set of shells; the sides of the upper part extend past the
cornice to help form "boxes" below the side finials; the boxes place
all the finials at the same level; they and the use of three rather than
two pediment plaques minimize the central focus that is part of the
Newport statement. Joseph Brown's brick house of 1774 at 50 South

FIG. 158 Commode, 1700–1710, Paris, France, decorative patterns in the style of Jean Bérain. Marquetry in *contre-partie* on an ebony ground; chased and gilt bronze mounts. Wallace Collection.

FIG. 159 Chest-on-chest, 1710–30, Holland or northern Germany. Woods unknown; japanned. Courtesy, Shreve, Crump and Low Co., Boston, Massachusetts.

Main Street, Providence, has a sweeping serpentine-shaped pediment cornice flanked by corner balustrades. Together they match the profile of the boxed and central arching top line of his desk and bookcase.

The nine-shell piece has recently been assigned an origin in Providence, rather than Newport, Rhode Island.[5] The easily discerned Providence features are the boxes on the top (they more normally appear on clock cases); the small half-round drops near the inner ends of the bracket feet; the quite plain desk interior; and the outer as well as the inner shells carved from the solid, with their upper edges recessed into the wood. Carving the convex shells from the solid can be understood as a willingness to do unnecessary labor as part of creativity, or as a less sophisticated shop practice. The extra features—four rather than three long drawers, three more shells, three panels in the pediment, boxes raising the side finials, the outer curves of the escutcheons on the desk lid being cut away so a large quantity of shining brass can be slid between the shells—add an interesting cluttering to the Newport look. This additive urge is not unrelated to how Connecticut makers reused Newport's clarified manner of handling the block-and-shell idea (compare figures 155 and 174; the Connecticut piece also has its bold shells carved from the solid).

In America, the blocked form appeared in New Hampshire, Massachusetts, Newport, New York, and Connecticut. (There are about three examples made in the South under the influence of imported blocked pieces.[6]) Since blocked facades continue to be called uniquely American by scholars and critics, even though I have published non-American examples,[7] I have included four examples of the form made in various parts of the Continent, where the configuration was used from Spain and

FIG. 160 Dressing table, 1715-25, probably northern Italy. Woods unknown. Robert Wemyss Symonds Collection of Photographs, Winterthur Library; Joseph Downs Collection of Manuscripts and Printed Ephemera.

Italy to Scandinavia, where it appeared on high-style pieces and those of painted pine. The shaping was not used in England. There, related articulated facades have much shallower projections, or, if bolder, the side sections are shaped to reverse curves. The bold form of the shaping was used on many pieces made in Paris about 1700 (figure 158). The blocked japanned chest-on-chest of about 1720 (figure 159) is from Holland or northern Germany. The probably northern Italian goat-foot dressing table of about 1720 (figure 160) has flat rather than the rounded blocking found on the previous examples. The German print by J.G. König (figure 161) of Augsburg, Germany, was published about 1740–50. Its basic shaping is slathered over with rococo decoration, but underlying the enrichment are features found on the Newport piece. They include shells capping the blocking and panels in each side of the pediment. The panels look like the applied panels on the pediment of the Newport desk and bookcase, and although fixed in place, they have the appearance of drawer fronts. On simpler and shorter related German pieces, such panels are often actual drawer fronts. The print shows turned feet as seen on the Newport desk and bookcase in figure 190.

Both of Newport's basic ways of handling form give an expansive sense of volume. One, using blocks and shells, has a baroque rolling surface and is found on a few desks and bookcases, some chests of

FIG. 161 Print of a desk and bookcase, 1740-50, by J. G. König, Augsburg, Germany. From Heinrich Kreisel, *Die Kunst des deutschen Möbels, Zweiter Band Spätbaroch und Rokoko* (Munich, 1970), fig. 1081.

FIG. 162 Roundabout chair, 1760-90, probably by one of the Townsend-Goddard families, Newport, Rhode Island. Mahogany, maple, and pine. The Rhode Island Historical Society.

drawers, and many chest-on-chests and their accompanying kneehole dressing tables. The roundabout armchair (figures 154 and 162) is a bold statement of such action. The form makes a strong and serviceable chair that provides support to the back and arms; here, they are recessed for elbow rests. When depicted in contemporary portraits, such chairs usually hold a sitter writing or reading at a table in the center of the room. This roundabout is one of a pair; the other retains its original leather seat covering. They were made for John Brown and may have stood with his desk and bookcase in the room seen as figure 154. Family tradition asserts that John Brown sat in one and George Washington in the other when Washington visited Providence.

Newport's other way to handle bold mass was to contain it in tight box-like units that showed little interruption to their surfaces. It was particularly appropriate for high chests and their accompanying dressing tables. The high chest (figure 163) creates a taut case of drawers placed on an equally restricted stand with drawers. The shell in the skirt is very close to the surface. (In other regions, skirt shells feel recessed into their drawers.) The flatness of the case's front and sides continues on to the legs. The drawer fronts, panels in the pediment, and brasses give some plasticity to the front.

The legs do not continue up to form the corners of the lower case. As shown as figure 88, the top part of the leg was reduced in size and fitted with glue blocks inside the corners of the lower case. A shallow strip of wood, using vertical grain, was inserted into the case above the legs so from the front, the wood of the legs seems to continue to the midmolding. That the side of the lower case has a shrinkage crack that goes all the way from corner to corner shows that the lower case was made like a box, with the legs placed inside.

Other features particular to Newport contribute to its sense of volumetric forms that are difficult to penetrate visually. Unlike in other regions, thin horizontal boards close the top by arching over it behind the cornice moldings. A board placed behind the central finial further closes the hood. That board on figure 163 is covered with fingernail marks from people wanting to understand its purpose. The most sculptural details of the high chest of drawers are the front feet: the tendons of the ankles continue into the claws, and the talons stand in full relief (figure 164). In America, the shaping is associated with Newport, and the practice was borrowed from Great Britain (figure 165). On London pieces, open talons were upon occasion made of ivory.[8] They also appear on pieces made in India for

FIG. 163

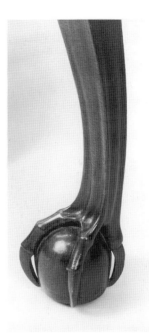

FIG. 164

FIG. 165

the English market.[9] (The idea of a claw-and-ball foot comes from China, where the concept was of a dragon's foot holding a pearl.[10])

Although the front legs have sculpted feet, those at the rear are lathe-turned. This is not because the piece is transitional between two styles; rather, it is a means of keeping the action to the front plane—and it did save money. Similarly, the urns of Newport finials usually have reeding only on their outer faces—their backs are plain.

The high chest has another feature found on most Newport two-part case pieces. In other regions, and on a few Newport pieces, the containing midmolding is nailed to the lower case, and the upper case rests inside it. The Newport practice nailed the midmolding to the upper case, and a downward projecting lip keeps the upper case from moving backward or from side to side. With this configuration, there is less chance of chipping the midmolding when the top section is placed on the lower part.

FIG. 163 High chest of drawers, 1750–90, Newport, Rhode Island. Mahogany, chestnut, eastern white pine, and white oak. Yale University Art Gallery, Mabel Brady Garvan Collection.

FIG. 164 Detail from figure 163.

FIG. 165 Claw-and-ball foot with open talons, 1730–80, England. Wood unknown. Robert Wemyss Symonds Collection of Photographs, Winterthur Library; Joseph Downs Collection of Manuscripts and Printed Ephemera.

FIG. 166

FIG. 167

FIG. 166 Chest-on-chest, 1760-85, possibly
by Thomas Affleck (d. 1795). Mahogany.
Courtesy, Sotheby's, New York.

FIG. 167 Chest-on-chest, 1770-90, Pennsylvania, probably Philadelphia. American
black walnut and yellow poplar. Employs
German cabinetmaking features including wedged dovetails and large wooden
pins as fasteners. Yale University Art
Gallery, Mabel Brady Garvan Collection.

A major difference between the two extremes in Newport's way
of handling masses was cost: blocked forms required more wood
and far more time. As we saw in Section 16, Philadelphia cut expense
not by altering the basic concept or movement of its chairs, but by
eliminating special features, and the same is true of its case pieces.
The majestic mahogany chest-on-chest (figure 166) was made for
the Loockerman family of Dover, Delaware, possibly by Thomas
Affleck, about 1770. It consists of three pieces: two cases of drawers
and a pediment, including the lattice work architrave, which lifts
off to allow for careful transportation. The horizontal action of
the drawers is contained by engaged fluted quarter columns on
both the upper and lower cases. The brasses are stylistically later in
form than those with full back plates behind the bail handles on
figure 163.

The chest-on-chest (figure 167) may be later in date because it
uses neoclassical ovals (without rococo flourishes) as part of its pulls.
While still featuring engaged fluted quarter columns, the piece was

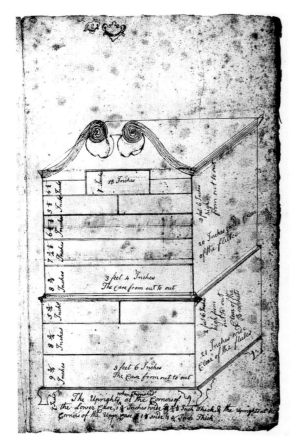

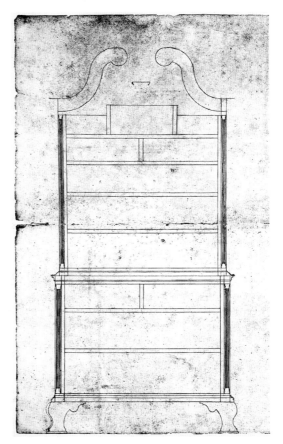

FIG. 168

FIG. 169

much cheaper to produce, for it has local woods, no pediment, and a simple cornice that is enriched only with dentils.

A few American eighteenth-century cabinetmaker's drawings are known, and they provide insight into shop practices. The drawings of the chest-on-chests, in figures 168 and 169, were probably made about 1766. (For an image of a "Plain Chair" from the same group of drawings, see figure 132.) The first shows the consciousness of laying out measurements; the second includes the vertical proportions associated with Philadelphia, and has engaged fluted quarter columns. The upper case sits in a two-part molding attached to the lower case. The chest-on-chest form was so practical it persisted through the next style period. Since the neoclassical stance preferred a sense of lightness, many of the large forms had their surface broken into smaller, smooth areas by the application of veneered panels that feature ovals and rectangles. These encouraged the eye to focus on the enrichments rather than on the overall mass.

London cabinetmakers produced high chests of drawers with turned legs from about 1690 to 1710 (figure 61), and a few with long cabriole legs between 1700 and 1730; and the form continued with some popularity in rural areas of England until about 1760.[11] But during most of the eighteenth century, sophisticated British patrons preferred the greater mass and practicality of chest-on-chests, and there, as in America, the form persisted well into the next century.

FIG. 168 Detail from a drawing of a chest-on-chest, ca. 1766, by Samuel Mickle and/or Jonathan Shoemaker, Philadelphia, Pennsylvania. Ink on paper. Philadelphia Museum of Art, Gift of Walter M. Jeffords.

FIG. 169 Drawing of a chest-on-chest, ca. 1766, by Samuel Mickle and/or Jonathan Shoemaker, Philadelphia, Pennsylvania. Ink on paper. Philadelphia Museum of Art, Gift of Walter M. Jeffords.

FIG. 170 Chest-on-chest, 1770–1810, England. Mahogany. Courtesy, Shreve, Crump and Low Co., Boston, Massachusetts.

FIG. 171 Drawing of a chest-on-chest, titled "A mahogany Chest upon d° [ditto]," dated August 1792, Gillows firm of Lancaster, England. Ink on paper. From Estimate books, Gillows of Lancaster papers, City of Westminster Public Library, London; author's photograph.

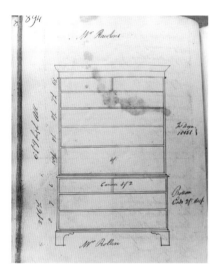

FIG. 171

FIG. 170

English scholars continue a preference for the chest-on-chest, and most fail to understand why America made and still appreciates the more open form with cabriole legs.

To continue the contrasting of related English and American work, I have included two examples of inexpensive English pieces. The simple English piece (figure 170) has neoclassical pulls and could have been made anytime between 1780 and 1810. The drawing (figure 171) is titled "A mahogany Chest upon d° [ditto]" and dated August 1792. It is one of thousands of drawings made by the Gillows firm, which was based in Lancaster, England. The Gillows sold furniture to customers throughout the British Isles, and by 1769 they had an outlet in London. In Section 25 we will see how some of their drawings of dining room tables help us understand the growing number of choices available to clients.

To finish this section, I want to look at how Connecticut borrowed from Newport's two ways of handling mass and turned them

into statements suitable for rural settings. (In the next section we will review how, after working for a few years in Philadelphia, a Connecticut cabinetmaker returned home and adapted what he had practiced in Philadelphia to make it appropriate for the homes of Connecticut patrons.)

The Newport chest-on-chest (figure 172) has the finely executed detailing that denotes a first-rate maker, possibly one of the Goddard or Townsend cabinetmakers. It was not inexpensive; it has a pediment and uses mahogany, rather than the cherry or maple those shops did employ. The customer chose not to add the cost of engaged fluted quarter columns, and the drawers have the easier-to-make lipped drawers, rather than cock beading attached to the sides of the drawers or the case around them. The form is tight: the bonnet is closed over the top and behind the center plinth. The midmolding is attached to the upper case.

FIG. 172 Chest-on-chest, 1750-90, Newport, Rhode Island. Mahogany, eastern white pine, and chestnut. Yale University Art Gallery, Mabel Brady Garvan Collection.

FIG. 173

FIG. 174

The Connecticut chest-on-chest (figure 173) uses Rhode Island features in the shaping of its pediment: cornice moldings, molded edges around the cutouts, fluted finial plinths, and applied panels. However, it does not close the pediment across the front or over the top, and it does not employ Rhode Island's brief, tightly twisted flame finials. The Connecticut finials are tall and even looser in movement than those made in Boston (figure 115). While the Rhode Island piece has a quiet upward movement established by graduated drawers and mounting brasses, the Connecticut piece stops the upward flow with a full sunburst in a central drawer. Massachusetts used central drawers, but there the carving was usually a fan shape, and its straight lower edge relates to the horizontal movement of the drawer below, while its arching top line echoes the movement of the cornice above (figure 111). On the Connecticut chest-on-chest, the sunburst's wavy outline is echoed in the outline of the central drop below the base molding. A further rural touch is found in the painting of the finials. The small balusters on the sides of the central plinth show their original light green paint; the finials have a later coat of dark green over the original light green. This piece has a sense of immediate presence. To move the eye up the front, the stripes of the tiger maple pattern change directions as they progress upward.

In contrast to the plain-style Connecticut chest-on-chest, figure 174 pushes Rhode Island's baroque movement, as found on the John Brown desk and bookcase (figure 155), into thundering action. There is no quiet consistency here: there are four kinds of shells; only the two that cap the outer parts of the blocking match. Unlike in Newport, they are carved from the solid, and the faces of their drawers have meandering incised lines above the shells. The bottom molding suspends four C-shapes. The corner decorations are fully rounded columns carved to a rope pattern. The pediment has dentils that alternate up and down between two rows. There are pinwheel rosettes and fanciful finials that disregard the tradition of an urn-shape support. This is a grand, new sculptural statement with exciting movements up and down the facade: if you begin at a lower corner you can go up the outer edge, around the top of a side shell, down to the base molding, around the lower shell, and up and down again.

FIG. 173 Chest-on-chest, 1770-90, North Stonington, Connecticut. Highly figured soft maple, soft maple, eastern white pine, and butternut; balusters in front corners of central plinth with light green paint; finials with dark green paint over light green. Yale University Art Gallery, Mabel Brady Garvan Collection.

FIG. 174 Chest-on-chest, 1770-90, Colchester, Connecticut, by Samuel Loomis (1748-1814). Mahogany, tulip poplar, and pine. Wadsworth Atheneum, Hartford, Gift of Mr. and Mrs. Arthur L. Shipman, Jr.

A Connecticut Maker's Transference of Philadelphia High-Style Forms

The Philadelphia high chest of drawers (figure 175) is one of America's richest statements and is easily related to the Philadelphia tea kettle on stand made in the same town by Joseph Richardson (figure 124). The pattern of the wood playing against the brasses, and the movement of the central cartouche, achieve as much asymmetry as any American shape of the period obtained. To make as much shimmering surface as possible from expensive, elaborately grained mahogany, the maker cut it into veneers. The normal practice was to surround veneered drawers with protective cock beading, which meant the backing wood did not show. This maker mounted the veneers as the outer faces of lipped drawers (except for the top right drawer front that has solid patterned mahogany, and the shell drawer front made of solid plain mahogany), which necessitated making the drawer fronts of mahogany.

The leafage on the drawer front and on the face of the pediment was made separately and glued and tacked in place. The leafage on the skirt is cut from the solid: below the drawers the surface was gradually sloped back, so the bottom leafage seems to project beyond the front plane.

The cherry high chest of drawers (figure 176) was made in the workshop of Eliphalet Chapin in East Windsor, Connecticut. He was trained in Connecticut, but, to escape a paternity suit, he spent four years (1767–71) working as a journeyman in Philadelphia. He opened a shop in East Windsor in 1771. His second cousin, Aaron Chapin, worked in Eliphalet's shop until 1783 when he moved to work in Hartford. Either or both men, or others in the shop, may have worked on the cherry high chest. From Philadelphia, Eliphalet brought the form of the cartouche, leaf-decorated cornice rosettes, pierced pediment, fluted quarter columns on both cases, and the shape of the skirt. The form of his feet is a bold version of the Philadelphia foot. On some Chapin-shop pieces, the shells on the center drawers are replaced by stylized leafage.

The high chest of drawers (figure 177) was made and labeled (figure 178) by the Philadelphia maker William Savery. He was

FIG. 175 High chest of drawers, 1760-85, Philadelphia, Pennsylvania. Mahogany, mahogany veneer, tulip poplar, and pine. Leaf-carved edges of rosettes made about 1939. Museum of Fine Arts, Boston, The M. and M. Karolik Collection of Eighteenth-Century American Arts.

FIG. 176

FIG. 176 High chest of drawers, 1771-95, East Windsor, Connecticut, workshop of Eliphalet Chapin (1741-1807). Cherry and white pine; sheet metal attaching back of cartouche to back of plinth; mid-twentieth-century finish. Winterthur Museum.

FIG. 177 High chest of drawers, 1760-85, Philadelphia, Pennsylvania, labeled by William Savery (1721-1788). Mahogany. Courtesy, Sotheby's, New York.

FIG. 178 Label of William Savery on figure 177. Courtesy, Sotheby's, New York.

FIG. 179 High chest of drawers, 1792-1801. Possibly by Julius Barnard (working 1792-1802), Northampton, Massachusetts. Cherry, white pine, and brass. Owned by Governor Caleb Strong of Northampton, Massachusetts. Historic Deerfield, Inc.

FIG. 177   FIG. 179

trained in the shop of Solomon Fussell, where he learned to make vernacular rush-seated chairs, as in figure 100. When on his own, he added high-style forms to his production, Since, according to the inventory of his shop, he did not own a set of carving tools, he probably purchased his ornamentation from a carving shop.[1] The high chest was made in three sections; the top lifts off just above the top drawers, making it easier to carefully move the piece. This was the first labeled Philadelphia high chest to be illustrated, and the discovery set the tone for understanding Philadelphia case furniture.[2] On the Chapin and the Savery high chests, the central ornament surmounts a rounded plinth.

FIG. 178

Eliphalet Chapin's transference of Philadelphia forms and motifs affected various local makers besides his cousin Aaron. Recent research attributes the high chest (figure 179) to Julius Barnard of Northampton, Massachusetts. He had trained in Eliphalet Chapin's workshop.[3] Its upper fan has a past-the-half-round profile of the Philadelphia rounded shell at the bottom of figure 175.

FIG. 180

FIG. 181

FIG. 180 Detail from high chest in figure 175.

FIG. 181 Cartouche from a high chest of drawers, 1771-95, workshop of Eliphalet Chapin (1741-1807). Cherry; pine extension to be slotted into fretwork and screwed to back of plinth; multiple maple braces applied to back to strengthen breaks. Wadsworth Atheneum, Hartford, Gift of Mr. and Mrs. Robert P. Butler.

Un-Philadelphia-like, figure 179 uses brass caps and stop-fluted bases on the quarter columns, a decoration usually associated with clock cases. The use of brass adds a delightful eccentricity that rural communities could enjoy.

To contrast the two cartouches, figures 180 and 181, is to compare two great, highly styled pieces of sculpture: one a sophisticated urban experience, the other an elaborate rural expression.[4]

To compare the Chapin side chair (figure 182) and the Philadelphia chair (figure 130) is to see again how Chapin adjusted Philadelphia details to suit a different situation. Chapin's back stiles have a greater angle as they move to the ears; the ears have a gentle rolling form as on the Massachusetts chair (figure 149), but Chapin placed a groove in their centers. Although on some chairs Chapin used a Philadelphia-style shell on the crest rail, alternating lobes and flutes (see figure 150), on this chair all the parts are positive lobes. Also, unlike standard Philadelphia practice, the strap work of the splat is organized as in New England to four supporting ribs below four C shapes that drop from the crest rail. The front feet are bolder versions of the Philadelphia foot. The most accurate use of Philadelphia features is where they are least visible: rounded back legs, through tenons, and corner blocks, originally only glued into place (as in figure 153), made of two pieces of vertically grained pine.

FIG. 182 Chair, 1771-95, East Windsor, Connecticut, workshop of Eliphalet Chapin (1741-1807). Cherry, white pine, and white oak; original webbing and primary seat covering. Yale University Art Gallery, Mabel Brady Garvan Collection.

The seat retains its original webbing and primary covering.[5] This and other Chapin chairs are unusual during this period in joining the back stiles to the crest rails with round, rather than flat, tenons.[6] During the ensuing period, this practice appeared on some neoclassical chairs.

The stance of the Chapin chair differs from the Philadelphia and the Massachusetts Chippendale chairs (figures 130 and 142) in its degree of visual activity: the back stiles thrust outward to the ears; the main straps of the splat sweep around in large curves.

The Value of a Trained Eye

In 1979 an auction catalogue described a table (figure 183) as though it were a provincial piece: "Queen Anne walnut tea table, rectangular top with molded edges, single drawer in the skirt . . . chestnut secondary wood. Provenance: the table descended through the Simeon Doggett family of Taunton, Massachusetts, and Rhode Island, 1740–1760." The estimate was $6,000–$8,000. It was bought for $29,150[1] by the New York firm of Israel Sack and priced there as a finely detailed Newport mahogany example at $45,000. Figure 184 is a Newport table with locally favored stop-fluted legs. Comparing the upper parts of the two tables (figure 185) makes a viewer stop and look more closely at the turned-leg piece. Both tables have clean, beautifully drawn, modestly shaped parts as found on the Newport dressing table in figure 87. Probably what threw the auction cataloguer was the turned feet on turned legs. They too easily suggested a Queen Anne date and a rural beginning. The detail of a foot (figure 186) is on a drawing made by the Gillows firm of the north of England and dated May 1793. The inscription above the foot reads: "the legs turned & round toes."

FIG. 184

FIG. 183 Table, 1740-90, Newport, Rhode Island. Mahogany and chestnut. Courtesy, Israel Sack, Inc., New York.

FIG. 184 Table, 1750-90. Newport, Rhode Island. Mahogany. Courtesy, Israel Sack, Inc., New York.

FIG. 185 Details from figures 183 and 184.

The table (figure 187), probably from Newport, uses the configuration on a beautifully shaped mahogany piece. Such legs and feet appear on countless English chairs and tables and many American pieces well into the next century. (The lathe-turning process for making such legs and feet is shown in figure 36.)

The instance of the miscalculation by the auction house points out how easy it is to let one or two factors denote an object's time or place. A trained eye will fully attend to details but will judge the piece on its allover character and quality.

Walking up to the table (figure 183) yielded two experiences, first when it was in a cluttered auction preview and later when it was grandly on display at Sack's in New York. From a distance, the front view—the space enclosed by the legs, the strong horizontal of the drawer with small keyhole and no pulls, and the slicing line of the wide top—added up to clarified beauty. When seen up close, the projecting top covered the drawer and most of the legs, and the sensation was of a crisply drawn, beautiful dark rectangle with finely molded edges.

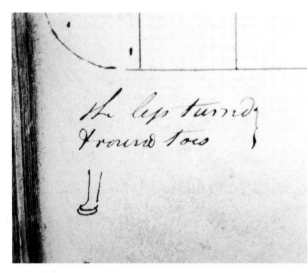

FIG. 186 Detail from a drawing showing a round foot, titled "the legs turned & round toes," dated May, 1793, Gillows firm of Lancaster, England. Ink on paper. From Estimate books, Gillows of Lancaster papers, City of Westminster Public Library, London.

FIG. 187 Drop-leaf table, 1740-90, Newport, Rhode Island. Mahogany. Courtesy, Israel Sack, Inc., New York.

FIG. 186

FIG. 187

Uniqueness, Rarity, and the Marketing of Newport Masterpieces in the 1990s

This section looks at three Newport case pieces that achieved record prices at auction. Although major pieces of Newport furniture were appreciated throughout the twentieth century by discriminating collectors, their rise to prominence began in the early 1950s. In 1953, there was a loan exhibition of Newport furniture held in the mid-eighteenth-century Newport Nichols-Wanton-Hunter House, which has wonderful paneling. A year later, Ralph E. Carpenter, Jr., who had curated the exhibition, published *The Arts and Crafts of Newport, Rhode Island, 1640–1820*, which included seventy-nine examples of Newport furniture; twenty-eight had been in the exhibition. The catalogue also pictured paintings and silver made in Newport. The exhibition and the catalogue brought greater attention to Newport furniture, and during the ensuing decade it began to be priced at a higher level.[1] The 1965 John Brown House Loan Exhibition of Rhode Island Furniture, held in that Providence house, confirmed Newport's aesthetic and thereby monetary value.

Until the 1970s, expensive pieces were usually purchased through dealers who bought at auctions, out of homes, and from other dealers who had made the initial contacts with owners. Major dealers rightly prided themselves on their depth of knowledge and the ability to contribute to building significant collections. When pieces began to bring hundreds of thousands of dollars, dealers could not as easily buy at auction for inventory. Today, they often have significant pieces in stock, but also regularly act as advisors and agents for collectors who can pay the really big prices.

In the mid-1970s, auction houses shifted from being primarily clearinghouses and entered the retail market by adopting marketing techniques developed in other businesses: they promoted themselves as primary sources for quality pieces. After the mid-1980s, catalogues, which had previously shown only a handful of black and white images, became fully illustrated, and in the late 1990s they moved to full color. For many years auction house personnel have arranged private sales between buyers and sellers of individual pieces when neither party cares to wait for an entire collection to come to

FIG. 188 Kneehole dressing table, 1760-90, Newport, Rhode Island. Mahogany. Courtesy, Sotheby's, New York.

auction, but since the 1980s auction houses have advertised their departmental experts as able to guide collectors to the best examples. In 1999, Christie's, the New York auction house, promoted itself as a new kind of museum when it moved to 20 Rockefeller Plaza. Its magazine's review of the celebrity opening included (partly in red lettering): "The museum where everything may be bought, known as '20 Rock' was definitely open for business . . ."[2]

Newport furniture was the first American expression to break through the $100,000 level: in 1969, the firm of Israel Sack sold a complexly carved block-and-shell dressing table, signed by Daniel Goddard, for $250,000; it had just been found in England.[3] The first three American pieces to break the $100,000 level at auction were all made in Newport. On January 17, 1967, a block-and-shell kneehole dressing table was bought by Doris Duke at Samuel T. Freeman & Co., in Philadelphia, for $102,000.[4] In 1971 she purchased the Hazard family high chest of drawers at Sotheby's in New York, for $104,000.[5] On October 21, 1972, Sotheby's sold a block-and-shell dressing table in the Lansdell K. Christie sale for $120,000. Eight years later the same piece brought $275,000 at auction.

A Florentine *pietra dura* ebony and ormolu cabinet holds the record, at $15,178,020, for the highest price paid to date for a piece of furniture at auction.[6] The Newport desk and bookcase in figure 189 is the second highest, and the Newport desk and bookcase, figure 190, is number three.

By reviewing three pieces of Newport furniture, I want to raise the question of trophy collecting, which pertains to objects for sale at any price. I am raising the issue of valuing a piece because it is the only one known or the only example with one or more particular features. Are the features present because of the client's ability to pay more; do the special features raise the object aesthetically above similar pieces that do not have them; did the client's asking for these features push the maker to create a masterpiece? It could be that certain features were not repeated because the maker or another client found them uninteresting. Another reason for a high price is that the example is the only one of a desirable group not in a public institution.

In 1996, the Mr. and Mrs. Adolph Henry Meyer sale included the block-and-shell kneehole dressing table (figure 188). The estimate provided in the catalogue was $800,000 to $1,200,000, and it brought $3,632,500. It is attributed to Edmund Townsend on the basis of its similarity to a piece in the Museum of Fine Arts, Boston, that retains his paper label.

The form served as a companion to chest-on-chests, just as more open dressing tables, or lowboys, were paired with high chests of drawers. (In the eighteenth century the more solid form of dressing table was called by a variety of names, among them "knee hole chest of drawers," "bureau table," and "bureau dressing table."[7]) As with the more open dressing table, the kneehole form does not provide much room for a sitter's knees. Contemporary paintings show owners sitting sideways to both forms, and the piece usually supports a looking glass. Everything is placed in front of a window so that during daylight hours, outside light can make the sitter's image easily visible in the looking glass.

The details of the kneehole dressing table are beautifully arranged: the edges of the projecting blocking begin as scrolls on the feet, then move up, in, and through the base molding, up the sides of the blocking, and around the shells. The outer lines of the recessed shell on the long drawer are carried down through the board below the drawer. The form of the recessed shell steps back to be used again on the cupboard door, where it caps a tall niche. The recess carries down through the base molding. There is a typical Newport cove molding between the case and the projecting top; together they give sufficient weight to the top line so it scales to the bold elements below.

The auction catalogue entry for this piece included "Retains its original patina." It also states that it is "apparently the only example of this rare form which has survived with its original finish." Undoubtedly, there is original finish under and mixed with the surface dirt. The question this piece raises, as we discussed in Section 3, is: What is the value of a finish on a high-style piece that obfuscates the concept of the maker? Dirt on a painted piece almost always means leaving it alone, for to clean is to diminish the quality of the painted surface. To carefully clean away dirty varnish—as with cleaning a painting—is to let the quality of the patina of the original intention show. Clearly no private collector will touch this piece; only a public institution not interested in resale would remove the varnish and revarnish. If the kneehole is ever cleaned, certain areas not easily visible must be left intact so researchers can always analyze patches as new questions about early finishes arise.

In 1989, the Nicholas Brown desk and bookcase (figure 189) sold for $12,100,000, the record for an American piece. (The agent buying the piece for one of his firm's active customers was authorized to go up to $20,000,000.[8]) Related examples were made for Nicholas's brothers John (figure 155) and Joseph (figure 157); the latter was produced in Providence.

There are a few related pieces, in private collections, where the bookcase has only two doors and each is enriched with one large shell, but the Nicholas Brown piece is the only one of the nine three-door examples left in private hands. Unless a museum that owns two of them (the Museum of Fine Arts, Boston, and the Museum of Art, Rhode Island School of Design, Providence) sells one, it is unlikely another will be available again. Thus the price for a major American statement.

FIG. 189 Desk and bookcase, 1760-90,
Newport, Rhode Island. Mahogany,
chestnut, white pine, maple, and cherry.
Courtesy, Christie's, New York.

The Nicholas Brown piece should be studied with the John
Brown example, which has dark mahogany containing the upper
case. The lock escutcheon plate on the top drawer of the Nicholas
Brown piece wraps up onto the face of the drawer so the lock's
keeper can go up into the rail above it. This placement of the upper
escutcheon gives an allover arching feeling to the brasses on all the
drawers. On the John Brown piece, the top escutcheon is placed
lower and the lock's keeper goes down into a drawer divider. On the
John Brown desk, the brass button pulls on the slide above the drawers are placed under the hinges; on the Joseph Brown piece they are
over the drawer pulls.

At 112 inches, the Nicholas Brown piece is the tallest of the group. Some find it too tall, while others find it marvelous. Aesthetic preferences are conditioned by experience, and in a late eighteenth-century tall-ceilinged room this height may seem logical. When Berry Tracy, then curator of the American Wing of the Metropolitan Museum of Art, saw the John Brown desk and bookcase, he said, "It's too tall," for he was intimately familiar with the one in his museum. At 99⅛ inches, it is about eight inches shorter than the John Brown piece (figure 155), and about 13 inches shorter than the Nicholas Brown example (figure 189). With this level of achievement, preference is the result of an individual's eye.

The surprise of the 1999 auction season was the Newport desk and bookcase made about 1750–60 by Christopher Townsend, who signed it three times in pencil. The auction estimate was $500,000 to $800,000, and it sold to an anonymous buyer for $8,252,500. The event garnered a two-page spread in the *New York Times,* where its history, discovery in Paris, and special features were described, and a minute-to-minute record of the bidding was given in detail (figure 190).

When sold, the piece was believed to have been first owned by the Boston family of Margaret and Nathaniel Appleton (1693–1784), for it descended in their family. It has rare, costly features, and why a Boston clergyman's family had such an expensive piece from Newport is unknown. It may have been made for their eldest son Nathaniel (1731–1798), a wealthy Boston businessman. It was taken to Paris, probably early in the nineteenth century, where it remained until it was shipped to be auctioned in New York. The rare features include the use of plum pudding (or mottled) mahogany, which gives the surface a depth of color and a kind of visual nervousness. It is unusual in having all the parts that are normally made of secondary woods employ mahogany. The interior of the desk area of the Nicholas Brown example uses mahogany as the secondary wood, but all-mahogany pieces are usually associated with tropical climates (for mahogany is less vulnerable than many woods to bug damage). Its use throughout figure 190, along with silver (even for the hinges), may show a determination to have the most expensive object possible. It is unique during this period in America in having silver loper and drawer pulls, escutcheons, and hinges, and they have the maker's mark of the Rhode Island silversmith Samuel Casey.

The lopers, or pulls, that support the desk lid when it is open, are the full height of the top drawer. In many Newport desks, they are of a square form (as in figure 189), which requires that the top

FIG. 190 Newspaper report on the sale of a desk and bookcase, signed in pencil three times by Christopher Townsend (1701-1773), Newport, Rhode Island; silver mounts stamped by Samuel Casey (1724-1780), Little Rest, Rhode Island; 1750-60. Primary and secondary woods, mahogany; ball feet not original (see text). From the *New York Times* (February 11, 1999), page B12.

FIG. 191 Interior of figure 190. Courtesy, Sotheby's, New York.

corners of the upper drawer fit around them. On this piece, the full-height lopers have silver parrots on their faces. Until the discovery of this desk and bookcase, parrots were known on Newport pieces in mahogany and brass. The bookcase section is unique in its inclusion of a classical tempietto, which features columns with Doric capitals (figure 191).

When viewed in Paris by the auction house representative, the desk had no ball feet, and the base molding looked too near the floor. The piece was not then tipped over so that the bottoms of what seemed to be bracket feet could be studied, and it was assumed that they had been shortened some inches. Upon the desk's arrival in New York, it was seen that the base of the existing brackets have square holes, and it was assumed they once held the square tenons of turned feet. (The holes are not cut into the bracket boards: the brackets create the outer faces of the square holes; the inner faces are supplied by glue blocks [figure 192]. Thus the construction to hold "removable" feet is rather like how Newport secured "detachable" legs [figure 88], where the upper extensions of the legs fit into the

corners of the lower case and are secured there by glue blocks.)
Turned feet at this date are unusual, although they exist on a few
contemporary American pieces and appear on the related German
piece depicted in the print seen as figure 161. There are turned
feet on a small valuables chest made and signed by Christopher's
son John Townsend, and they were
scaled up to become the pattern for
the new ball feet seen in figure 190.[9]

FIG. 192 Bottom of a bracket foot on figure 190. Courtesy, Sotheby's, New York.

Because it appeared that brackets
had not been cut down, the auction
house could avoid the detrimental
designation "feet cut down," and
instead praise the wonders of turned
feet on an American piece of this
date. The promoting of replaced
turned feet of uncertain shape over
predictable extensions of brackets
raises an interesting question. If
they had been reverse-curve feet (as
on figure 189), and they had been
shortened, their exact profile would
not be known. But where the brack-
ets have straight outer edges, and the inner curves have been com-
pleted, a simple downward extension is easy; only the height is
in question. If given the choice, would it not have been better to
simply extend the bracket feet, rather than to create turned feet
whose size and profile is not certain, although turned feet add
another unique feature?

A few months after the auction, the new owners temporarily
put the piece on display in the Philadelphia Museum of Art. It was
shown sitting on its brackets while research was done to decide if it
originally had turned or bracket feet. If the former, what were their
size and shape? If original bracket feet had been cut down, how tall
should they be?

Each piece in this section is deserving of great attention, and
their prices are not surprising. Just to stir the imagination and emo-
tions, which piece would you rather have at home or available in a
museum: one or all of these three Newport pieces; the Philadelphia
high chest of drawers (figure 175); the John Brown desk and bookcase (figure 155); the Boston bombé chest of drawers (figure 109);
one of the other high-style pieces included here? Or, do you prefer
less exquisitely finished pieces, even the in-the-rough dressing table
(figure 90)?

Two Phases of the Federal Period

In 1966, Charles F. Montgomery published American Furniture: The Federal Period, *which included about five hundred objects made between about 1780 and 1830 and owned by the Winterthur Museum. By using the term "federal," he was in part trying to introduce a designation that would replace the long-standing and grossly over-simplifying assignment of pieces made about 1800 to either the Hepplewhite or the Sheraton style. He gave the following reason for using "federal": "In Philadelphia, and perhaps elsewhere, furniture was made by 'The Federal Society of Cabinetmakers,' and many pieces of the period were carved or inlaid with the American eagle, symbol of the Federal union." He went on to explain that the term also worked for those pieces that embodied the classical ideal that employed Greek and Roman sources.[1] In ratifying the designation, Montgomery helped to create a new classification, but by using an overriding term to cover fifty years he obscured that during the time there were several rapidly evolving and competing styles to tempt buyers who ever more quickly demanded the new. The use of "federal" for these years has since been justified by finding it appropriate for a nation that became a federation of states in 1787, but the country is still united as a federation. The term is as inappropriate as Queen Anne—which covers three styles—and Chippendale, when he was but one of many London designer/makers working at the time. But until Americanists adopt radical changes in terminology, the now established designation communicates a time that focused on antiquity. I will discuss the two main styles of the federal period and emphasize their differences: the neoclassical or intellectual phase and the ensuing Greco-Roman styling. A more complex typology is possible and, in a longer study, probably preferable.*

The Renaissance had looked to ancient Greece and Rome for rational sources, and with adjustments its ordered forms continued into baroque classicism, which created heavy and vigorous architectural monuments and equally forceful furniture. At the beginning of the eighteenth century there was a new preference among some architects to reference a simpler classicism. This Palladian movement was initiated by the publication in 1715 of the first volumes of two books. Colen Campbell's Vitruvius Britannicus *showed classical buildings in England, among them works by Inigo Jones, who had been the principal architect to introduce Renaissance-style architecture into England early in the seventeenth century. The second was an English translation of a book by Andrea Palladio, the greatest northern Italian architect of the Renaissance. The illustrations in his* I quattro libri dell'architettura *show a purity and spareness of mass with flat, even severe, use of ornamentation and a "quest for absolutes and can thus be identified with the Age of Reason."[2] Inigo Jones had himself been influenced by the publication of Palladio's* Four Books of Architecture.[3] *The Palladian style was forwarded by Colen Campbell, Lord Burlington, and Burlington's life companion William Kent (an architect, painter, and designer of furniture, interiors, and landscapes).*

In the third quarter of the eighteenth century, there was another fresh look at the antique. The Enlightenment focused on Greece and Rome as sources for models of society and politics in which the rule of law and reason flowed from responsible individuals rather than hereditary leaders. The architects and designers were influenced by Palladio's simple

FIG. 193 Sofa, 1790–1810, Salem, Massachusetts.
Mahogany and hard maple. Yale University Art
Gallery, Mabel Brady Garvan Collection.

styling, but traveled to Italy and Greece to look firsthand at the antique. What resulted was an intellectual classicism that created idealized shapes: tight squares, rectangles, ovals, and circular forms that were enriched by thin layers of classical references (figure 193). (Originally, the severity and firmness of the sofa would have been somewhat relieved by cushions across the back.) The look was introduced into America about 1785. By 1805 in America, the second phase of the new developments saw designers create more archaeologically correct versions of objects used in Greece and Rome (figure 194).

To create what I am calling the neoclassical or intellectual phase, Continental and English designers such as Robert Adam often spent years in Italy studying ancient architecture, its surface treatments, and a variety of smaller artifacts. Other designers who visited Greece, as well as Rome, announced themselves to potential clients as not having confined themselves to Italy. After returning to England in 1758, Adam became one of England's most important architects and interior designers as he fashioned new buildings and reworked existing structures until his death in 1792. In his interiors, he broke up spaces with columns, and enriched walls with ovals, rectangles, swags, and other classical shapes. He distributed his themes and motifs throughout the entire room to make everything work en suite: the architectural details, furniture, and smaller objects. Even the pattern and colors of the carpet often matched the architectural moldings and colors of the ceiling.

Such court-level designs began to alter stately houses in the 1760s and the approach filtered down to merchant-level patrons by the mid 1780s, when two designers produced pattern books that would firmly condition the look of less expensive but fashionable furniture during the ensuing decades. George Hepplewhite's widow Anne Hepplewhite published his The Cabinet-Maker and Upholsterer's Guide *in 1788. It was published again the following year with slight revisions, and in 1794 an "improved" third edition appeared. Thomas Sheraton produced his* The Cabinet-Maker and Upholsterer's Drawing-Book *between 1791 and 1793, and it was issued in revised versions into the next century. These publications broadcast the new tightly contained forms with neoclassical motifs far beyond Britain, and became the first pictorial sources used widely in America. Earlier, such designers as Thomas Chippendale had in a more modest way shared London's ideas with a broad market, but none had the impact of these works.*

In Chippendale's third edition of the Director *in 1762, the old-style classicism is evident in the use of straight legs (echoing classical pilasters) as alternatives to cabriole legs, and dentil shapes employed as feet. Chippendale reflected the new Palladian classicism in his employment of square-tapered legs joined above by swags and ended in block feet—a look that became standard in both Hepplewhite and Sheraton designs. By the early 1760s, some of the pieces produced in Chippendale's furniture establishment were based on designs by Robert Adam. By the late 1760s, Chippendale was providing his own neoclassical designs.*

The new Hepplewhite and Sheraton books produced just the right degree of complexity in objects scaled to suit the needs of the merchant class in England and the upper and middle levels of American society, as makers applied shallow carving and inlaid or painted motifs to simple geometric forms. There was a happy confluence in that just as this taste was available from Europe, America was ready to set aside old forms and symbols and embrace new ones that spoke of the classical era.

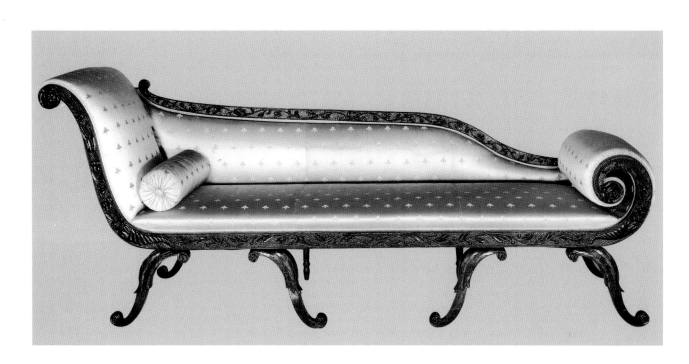

FIG. 194. Sofa, 1805-15, Salem, Massachusetts.
Mahogany and birch. Winterthur Museum.

The Neoclassical Style

The new unyielding tightness of form and detail is seen in the 1789 drawing of a Philadelphia house by the Boston architect Charles Bulfinch (figure 195). The house resulted from a stay in London by Anne Bingham, who asked the London architect John Plaw to develop the plans. Although this London design built in Philadelphia had little immediate effect on that city's architecture, it did affect how Charles Bulfinch would build in Boston; see, for example, his first Harrison Gray Otis house of 1795–96.[1] The simple mass of the Philadelphia house is broken into three horizontal bands. The center is marked by a rusticated doorway surmounted by a Palladian window below a lunette window. The facade is further enriched by four plaques that reference classical details, and the windows are capped only with a keystone.

New technology contributed to and was caused by the new classical taste. Rolled sheets of silver became widely available, and they could be formed into tight, severe shapes as seen in the coffeepot (figure 196). Its large urn form is topped by decreasing concave actions that terminate in an urn-form finial. Bright-cut decoration in the forms of an oval, swags, and leafage enriches the surface, and beading enhances the edges. All these small accents cause light to flicker across and around the smooth surface.

The card table (figure 197), probably made in Boston, is similarly tight. Everything is thin, shimmering, and on the surface. Not since the veneering of William and Mary case pieces had there been so little in-and-out play to uncarved flat surfaces. The rectangular top and its frame have recessed quarter-round front corners. The plane of the front of the frame is flush with the tops of the front legs, and their surfaces have flat, inlaid decoration: an eagle, below eighteen stars within a pointed oval, surrounded by an inlaid rectangle with re-entrant corners, marks the center of the frame. Urns

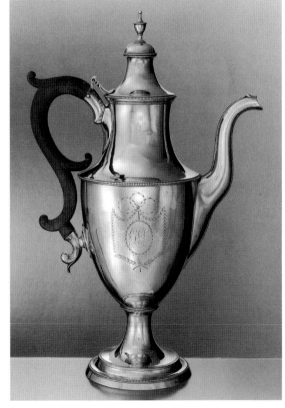

FIG. 196

FIG. 195 Drawing of Bingham House, Philadelphia, Pennsylvania, 1789, by Charles Bulfinch (1763-1844). Ink on paper. Courtesy, Library of Congress.

FIG. 196 Coffeepot, 1790-1800, Philadelphia, Pennsylvania, by John Germon (working ca. 1782-1816). Silver. Marked "Germon" and "Philad·" in rectangles on edge of foot. Yale University Art Gallery, Mabel Brady Garvan Collection.

FIG. 197 Card table, 1790–1810, Boston,
Massachusetts, area. Mahogany, mahogany veneer, various inlays, eastern
white pine, and birch. Yale University Art
Gallery, Mabel Brady Garvan Collection.

FIG. 198 Sideboard, 1790–1810, New York,
New York. Mahogany, mahogany veneer,
various inlays, pine, and tulip poplar;
blue and white enameled pulls. Museum of
Fine Arts, Boston, The M. and M. Karolik
Collection of Eighteenth-Century American Arts.

FIG. 197

FIG. 198

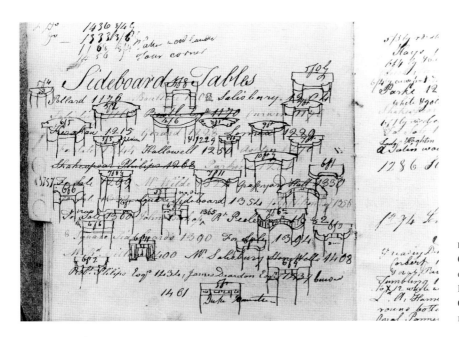

FIG. 199 Drawing of "Sideboard Tables," Gillows firm of Lancaster, England. Page cxii of the 1795-98 Index of the Estimate Book. Ink on paper. From Estimate books, Gillows of Lancaster papers, City of Westminster Public Library, London.

within pointed ovals enhance the tops of the legs. The decorative stringing in the edges of the two-part top, lower edge of the rail, and the ankle bands—like the bright cutting and beading on the silver coffeepot—add sparkling linear accents. Below the cuffs, the legs, in a New England fashion, taper more rapidly to form feet, which seems to place the piece on tiptoe.

The New York sideboard (figure 198) takes a giant serpentine-front mass and breaks it into discernible units by using the upper part of the center legs to divide the front into a swelling center and concave ends. The cupboard area of the center section is recessed, and on either side of the doors the surfaces curve quickly out to the legs. The legs are extraordinary: at the top they follow the curve of the serpentined drawer level; at the cupboard level they follow the concave faces of the ends. Those faces are carried down as the main surface as the legs taper almost to points. Below the case, the sides of the legs that face the center are straight from front to back. The piece uses inlaid stringing to create squares and rectangles around flashing veneers. The keyhole surrounds on the four cupboard doors are shaped to urns; the enameled drawer pulls have white urns on a blue ground.

The multiple drawing (figure 199) shows variations on the theme of a tight box on spindly legs. It was executed in the 1790s as one of thousands of drawings made by the Gillows furniture firm of Lancaster, England, who sold middle-level to stylish furniture with a provincial gloss throughout the British Isles. Most of the forms in this drawing use recessed positive or negative curved front corners, and straight end and back edges. A few have curving back lines to fit into curved architectural spaces. One is totally straight across the front; another is a half-circle table. All the forms could have been made in America, although here the curving back line was not common.

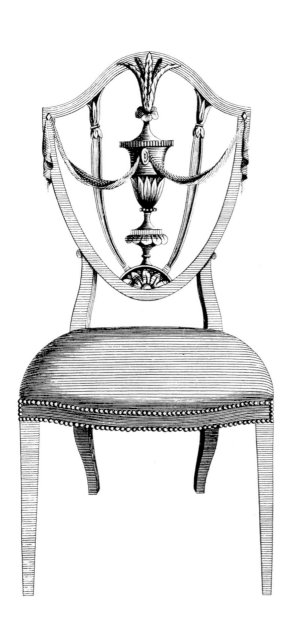

Neoclassical Chairs

The five New England chairs in this section are typical of the containing forms of 1790 to 1810. There is no breaking out into space except for the Windsor, which has splayed legs to provide the stability expected of a serviceable object, but they are rather more vertical than on Windsors from the preceding periods. The first three chairs accept a degree of vulnerable construction not seen since the William and Mary style put large cases of drawers and chair seats on spindly legs (figures 62 and 67).

The form of the published Hepplewhite design (figure 200) has no source in antiquity but is a compilation of ancient parts and motifs. The chair uses a shield-shaped back enhanced by an urn, swags, and other small classical patterns; the shape of the back is truncated for the outline of the seat. It joins an intellectual ideal of perfection with a careful reference to the origins of reason and the importance of the individual. Figure 201 shows a Salem, Massachusetts, interpretation of the published design. It has a history of belonging to the very successful Salem merchant Elias Hasket Derby. Like other pieces from his house, and Salem in general, it has references to grapes. The projecting parts of the spade feet are made of thin sheets of ebony glued onto the faces of the legs. Its style of carving is generally attributed to Samuel McIntire of Salem, an architect and carver who worked for the Derbys. Its constructional vulnerability comes from the forms of the parts of the back: the back stiles are one piece of wood from the floor to the top rail, a fairly sound use of the straight grain of the wood. The top rail has horizontal grain, and the serpentine-shaped piece can be easily broken through its serpentined curves. The same is true for the two horizontally grained, curving boards that form the lower part of the shield. (The English print source suggests a rounded one-piece line rather than a pointed two-piece lower shape, which would have been nearly as fragile.) There is an elegant movement of the back stiles of the Massachusetts chair as they curve in from the floor and up to support the shield. For the sitter, there is no comfort of a reverse-curve splat, as found in many Queen Anne chairs, nor the slight support of the backward-bowing

FIG. 200 Printed design for a chair, from *The Cabinet-Maker and Upholsterer's Guide,* by George Hepplewhite, 1788, plate 2. From reprint of third edition (New York: Dover Publications, 1969).

FIG. 201 Chair, 1790-1810, Salem, Massachusetts, carving possibly by Samuel McIntire (1757-1811). Mahogany, ash, birch, and possibly maple; ebony veneer on faces of front feet. Museum of Fine Arts, Boston, The M. and M. Karolik Collection of Eighteenth-Century American Arts.

of some Chippendale chair backs. Constructional logic and human comfort have been sacrificed to a visual need. Such pieces were still arranged around the circumference of a room, where they served as enrichments on the walls when not brought out to function at a card table or elsewhere.

The Massachusetts sofa (figure 193) has carving that relates it to Salem, and the piece provides one of the great stories about fakes. Much of the extraordinary Mabel Brady Garvan collection in the Yale University Art Gallery is in a basement store room where one can study closely adjacent pieces. When I was working there on the collection, Albert Sack called from New York to ask about "the Garvan McIntire sofa" that Garvan had put in his 1931 sale. For financial reasons, he had consigned a group of pieces not given to Yale to a New York auction house. Sack had been to see what was reported to be the auctioned sofa in a western collection. It had with it a small square of the textile that was on it in the auction catalogue—the same textile that is on it in figure 193. He was calling because he questioned the authenticity of the piece and wanted to know if I knew anything about it. I said, "It's about thirty feet away from me." I went and looked under the sofa and could see where a square of the textile had been removed. The auctioned sofa was not in a western collection but at Yale. Looking into the matter, it appears the following happened. Garvan sent the sofa to auction, the buyer took it away and copied it, kept a swatch of the textile, returned the sofa to the auction house "for nonpayment," and sold the copy into the western collection with a swatch of the textile that had appeared on the sofa in the catalogue. Garvan then sent the returned sofa to Yale.

FIG. 202 Chair, 1790-1815, history of being found in New Hampshire. Birch, walnut and fruitwood inlays, rush seat. Old Sturbridge Village.

The New England birch chair (figure 202) has a New Hampshire history. It is sturdy in its parts: there are stretchers, and in a rural manner the medial one has been moved out between the front legs. The spokes of its back are less breakable; the thickness of the lower parts of the shield make them less vulnerable. The rush seat, which probably supported a cushion, is a tough form of seat covering. The back stiles have over time shrunk in width, and, as discussed in Section 2, their original flowing unity with the top rail in forming a smooth-shaped shield has been lost: the top rail now projects past the outer faces of the stiles. Despite the chair's boldness, it has a careful attention to details: there is a bead molding on the outer corners of the front legs, the stiles above the seat, and the top rail. The partial patera, or arched base for the ribs, alternates light and dark woods.

Until the Renaissance introduced ordered units that employed naturally colored woods (figure 41), paint had articulated and en-

FIG. 203 Chair, 1790–1810, probably
Salem, Massachusetts, possibly Philadelphia, Pennsylvania. The shaping of the
back legs suggests Massachusetts. Maple,
cherry, oak, and pine, vertically grained
quarter-round glue blocks; white paint
with polychrome decoration; faces of front
feet applied. George M. and Linda H.
Kaufman Collection.

riched wooden surfaces. Highly styled William and Mary case pieces
employed rich veneers with legs painted to suggest ebony (figure 62),
while often that style's smaller pieces, such as banister- and slat-back
chairs, were painted. Fashionable furniture of the Queen Anne and
Chippendale periods was made with walnut and then later with mahogany. With the advent of the neoclassical style, there were two
ways to handle the surfaces of highly styled pieces. The flashing grain
patterns of mahogany remained popular, and for the first time the
natural color of light-colored woods, such as maple and birch, was
exploited. The second manner of handling high-style surfaces was
to paint the object and then apply fanciful painted decoration. Both
could be used in a high-style house but usually in different rooms.
Figure 203 is one of a number of painted chairs made for the Derby
mansion in Salem. The construction of the oval back is without cabinetmaker logic. It cuts circular shapes from boards and seems to ask
for breakage; it certainly demands stringent behavior from any sitter. (There is no evidence that the seat rails of this set had decorative

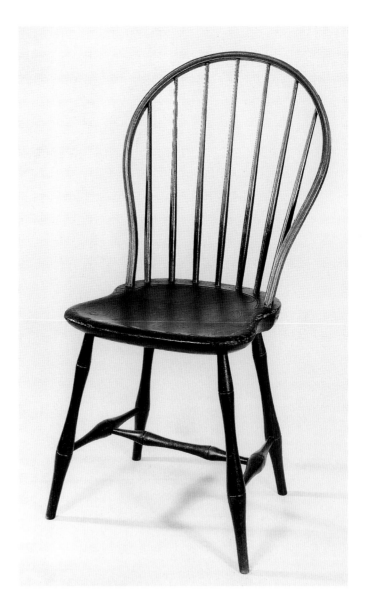

FIG. 204 Chair, 1800-1810, possibly
Connecticut River Valley. Ash, basswood,
and soft maple; layers of red, gray, green,
and then black paint. Yale University Art
Gallery, Mabel Brady Garvan Collection.

brass nails, as is found on most chairs of this period when the upholstery covers the rails.[1])

The bow-back Windsor side chair (figure 204) superbly uses the
character of wood in creating a vertical, lean stance with a swooping
circular back line. Its steam-bent top rail carries the line up from
the seat and then around beautifully shaped spokes. Unlike the active
saddle-seat shape on figure 14, this neoclassical chair's seat has a
quiet, circular movement that echoes the line of the back. There is
bamboo turning on the slender legs and stretchers. That the medial
stretcher has bamboo shaping, rather than a central swelling, places
it late within its type. There are traces of red, gray, and green under
the worn black paint.[2] Windsors are often hard to regionalize since
so many were sold away from where they were produced, and these
affected the look of local products. "The Windsor seat plank is often
the key to identifying the regional origin of a chair," and the use of
basswood for the seat suggests a Connecticut Valley origin, although
it was also employed in central Massachusetts, Rhode Island, and

along the northern New England coast. The central molding in the front face of the enclosing top rail is associated with Windsor chairs made in Boston.[3]

The Boston chair (figure 205) integrates a playfully neoclassical oval and two demi-ovals into a soundly constructed squared back; it is marked at its corners by applied flower-carved dies. Typical of many Boston and Boston-area neoclassical pieces, it exploits the possibilities of light-colored maple: much of the chair is of plain maple; the stretchers and ovals use solid tiger maple; the broad upper bands of the seat rails have cross-banded tiger maple veneer; the anklets above the New England–style tapered feet and the lower band of the seat use darker tiger maple veneer; and the four straight edges of the back and the front faces of the front legs are inlaid with bird's-eye maple veneer.

FIG. 205 Chair, 1790–1810, Boston, Massachusetts. Maple and birch. George M. and Linda H. Kaufman Collection.

The Late Neoclassical Look: Greater Mass and Movement

These two Portsmouth, New Hampshire, dressing tables show the shift to bolder, less stringent forms that began in America about 1805 and increased to voluminous extremes by the 1820s. The first (figure 206) has a taut bowed case visually lifted by the arching of the skirt, the tapering of the legs, and the greater tapering of the feet below inlaid cuffs. The front face of the case is veneered, and the cross-banded edges of the drawers take advantage of the light color of the sap wood of the veneer to introduce a flickering across their surfaces. The inlaid husks, or bellflowers, provide decreasing brightness as they narrow in size down the legs.

The dressing table (figure 207) is about fifteen to twenty years later. The boldness of the legs visually push the side drawers in. The center curves out, and its lower arch relieves the mass without providing lightness to the form. The larger drawer pulls are scaled to the greater weight of the turned elements. On its top is a case holding a bow-front drawer. It is held in place by round tenons projecting down from the turned corner posts.[1] The all-mahogany looking glass, resting on the small case, has been long associated with this dressing table. Since it has a generic form and no secondary wood, it is impossible to tell if it was made in England or New England until an identical piece with documentation appears.

FIG. 206 Dressing table, 1795–1810, Portsmouth, New Hampshire. Mahogany, rosewood and light wood veneers, and pine. Museum of Art, Rhode Island School of Design, Bequest of Charles L. Pendleton, by Exchange.

FIG. 207 Dressing table and dressing glass, 1810–30. *Dressing table, including ball-foot box with drawer:* Portsmouth, New Hampshire; mahogany, mahogany veneer, and pine; brass pulls. *Dressing glass:* Portsmouth or England; mahogany. Strawbery Banke Museum, Gift of Gerrit van der Woude.

FIG. 207

781

Messrs Van Aes   Wm Getskell
                                                                N.^o

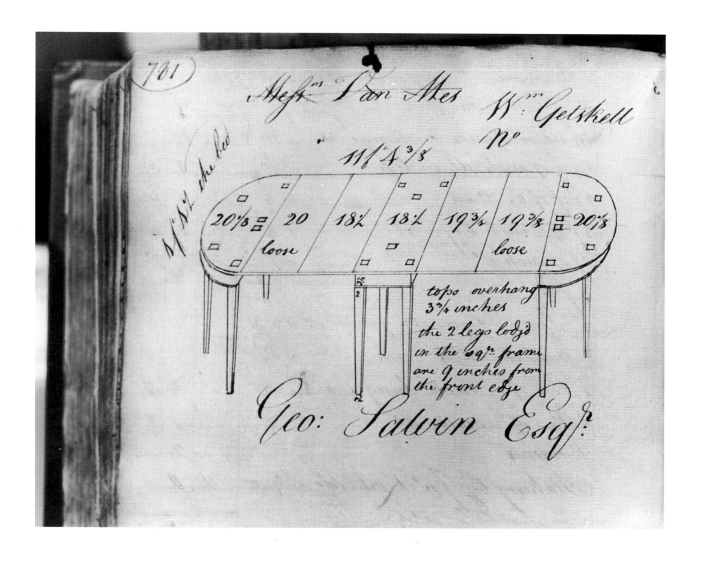

9 ft 10½ the bed

11ft 4 ³/₈

20⅞   20   18½   18½   19½   19⅞   20⅞
      loose   loose

tops overhang
3¾ inches
the 2 legs lodg'd
in the sq.^r frame
are 9 inches from
the front edge

Geo: Salvin Esqr

Multi-Part Dining Tables

Before moving to the Greco-Roman style, I want to review six drawings from the thousands produced by the Gillows firm of Lancaster, England. They show the ever-growing variations of forms and combinations of parts available to an expanding middle-class market that sought a greater range of objects. Before the neoclassical period, there was no specific room for dining, which occurred on drop-leaf tables that normally sat against a wall until they were set up for use in any one of a number of domestic spaces. Neoclassical houses gained a dining room that might be appointed with a new-fashion sideboard and a multi-part table. Its sections could be used separately: a drop-leaf table for dining and the shaped ends left against the walls as side tables, or the parts could be joined for a larger occasion. Today the parts are usually thought of as they appear in figure 208. The squares on the top of the half-round ends and the middle rectangular part designate the tops of the legs. The rounded ends had four fixed legs following their curve, and two swing legs at the center of their straight edge that opened to support the "loose" leaves. (The tapers of the swing legs are not depicted.) The center table had two swing legs about a foot in from each end (one of the tapered swing legs is shown). What is surprising about the drawing is the irregularity of the width of the parts—perhaps this was to maximize the widths of the boards available. Today, in our machine-perfect age, we would not tolerate such variations. Upon finding the tables in a house, shop, or museum, anyone would ask if they had been altered since they were made in 1791.

Figure 209 shows that you could get a center table with two leaves, a round end with a leaf, and one without. Perhaps this was a way to save money in a smaller room. When against a wall, the

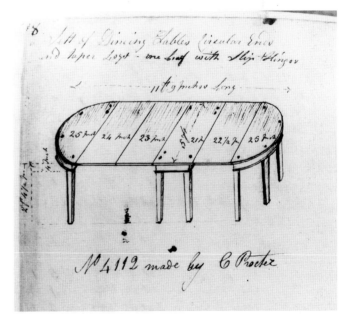

FIG. 209

FIG. 208 Drawing of a set of dining tables, dated October 1791, Gillows firm of Lancaster, England. Ink on paper. From Estimate books, Gillows of Lancaster papers, City of Westminster Public Library, London, page 781.

FIG. 209 Drawing of a set of dining tables, titled "Sett of Dining Tables Circular Ends and tapered Legs—one leaf with Slip Hinges," date unknown. Ink on paper. From Estimate books, Gillows of Lancaster papers, City of Westminster Public Library, London.

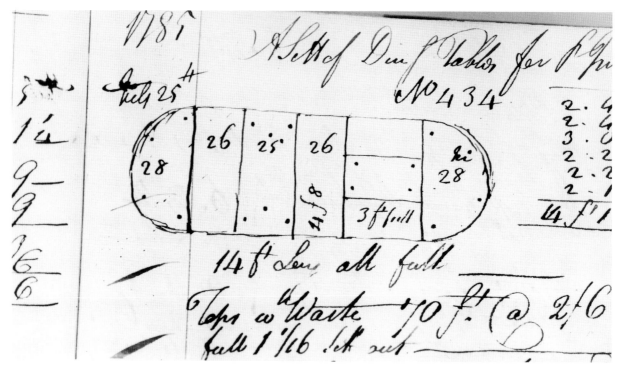

FIG. 210

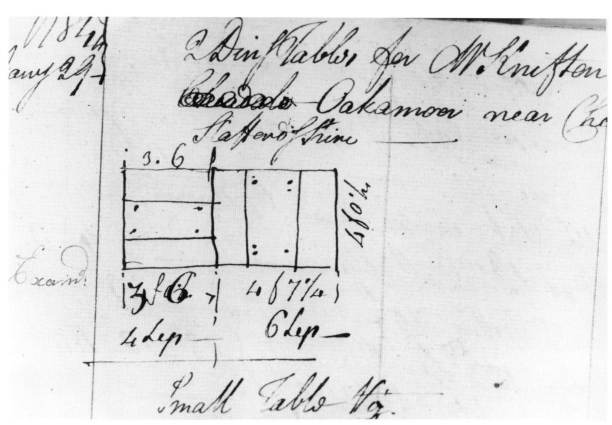

FIG. 211

FIG. 210 Drawing of a set of dining tables, titled "A Sett of Din[in]g Tables . . . ," dated July 1785, Gillows firm of Lancaster, England. Ink on paper. From Estimate books, Gillows of Lancaster papers, City of Westminster Public Library, London, page 212.

FIG. 211 Drawing of two dining tables, titled "2 Din[in]g Tables . . . ," dated January 1784, Gillows firm of Lancaster, England. Ink on paper. From Estimate books, Gillows of Lancaster papers, City of Westminster Public Library, London, page 9.

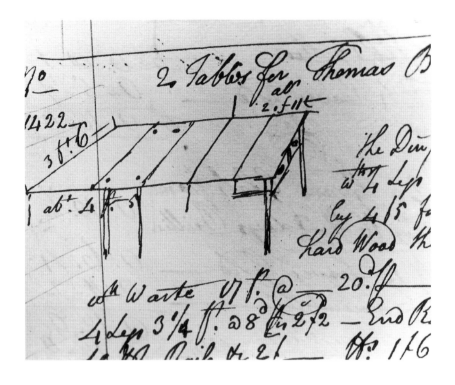

FIG. 212 Drawing of two tables, titled "2 Tables . . . ," table at left called "The Din[in]g Table"; table at right described as "The other Table wth one leaf & 2 draws," with "Round Handles"; dated April 1786; Gillows firm of Lancaster, England. Ink on paper. From Estimate books, Gillows of Lancaster papers, City of Westminster Public Library, London, page 329.

round ends would seem to match, and when in use no one would notice.

Figure 210 has circular ends without drop leaves, and there are two drop-leaf tables; one is much smaller than the other and is turned a quarter turn. The full width of the combined tables is shown as "4 f[eet] 8 [inches]." The small table is marked as being "3 f[eet] full" in width. This would give you two half-circular side tables, a regular and a small drop-leaf form.

Figure 211 is titled "2 Din[in]g Tables." One is 3 feet 6 inches in width with "4 legs" (there would have been brackets to pull out from the side rails to support the leaves, or two of the four legs could have swung as gates to support the leaves). The other table was "4 f 0" wide and it had "6 legs"; two would swing to support open leaves.

The two tables in figure 212 make me think of a combination suitable for New York apartment living. A drop-leaf table accompanies a card table with two drawers in the front facade shown at the right.

The 1791 drawing (figure 213) shows a square-tapered leg drop-leaf form at the center. It is combined with round ends that have the pedestal-type base normally associated with the subsequent era: a post supported by three cabriole legs. Most observers, upon seeing such a combination today, would ask if the ends had been made later.[1]

FIG. 213 Drawing of a set of dining tables, dated August 1791, Gillows firm of Lancaster, England. Ink on paper. From Estimate books, Gillows of Lancaster papers, City of Westminster Public Library, London, page 760.

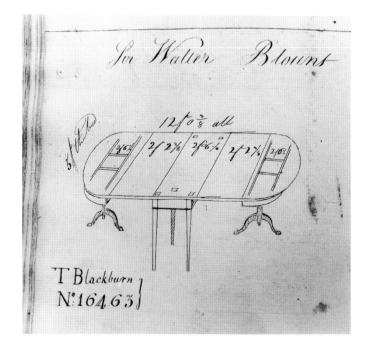

The Greco-Roman Style

The cool clarity of neoclassicism, with its precise, often decorative edges around smooth surfaces, had been used in all the arts, including furniture, silver, and dress. In Europe during the 1770s, men and women's clothing hugged the body so its natural shapes could be displayed like those of weather-bleached antique statues. The yardage in a woman's dress was reduced by about two-thirds and was often of statue-white material so thin it clung revealingly. The fronts of men's coats were cut away and "The torso and legs were displayed in an un-broken line, from ribcage to calf." The intent was "to present the body as nearly 'natural' as could be acceptably allowed."[1] On occasion, when men's tight-fitting pantaloons were peeled off, the impression of a corded textile was left in the flesh.[2] By 1805, classical references in clothing, as in furniture, were more picturesque. In the Thomas Sully portrait of 1818 (figure 214), the dress drapes off the shoulder. The previously severe neckline (as on the earlier dress in figure 226) is softened with lace, puff sleeves replaced those that clung to the upper arm, and the lower limbs are less evident. The harp—while much larger than those in antiquity—and the Arcadian landscape denote an idealized classical setting. The shawl, a fashionable accessory since the 1770s, is picturesquely draped.[3] The white dress is surrounded by earth tones, and the brighter colors are muted.

While the Boston area had featured light-colored woods during neoclassical styling, New York had preferred rich, dark mahogany, and the town continued this preference into the Greco-Roman style. When I first encountered the card table in figure 215, I rejected it as not being a good furniture design. As a cabinetmaker, furniture designer, and scholar of earlier material, I preferred forms that express the nature of wood. Queen Anne and Chippendale pieces have knee brackets that firm up the knee joints while continuing the lines of the legs through to the horizontals of the rails. Even with neoclassical forms, there is a smooth integration of the surface of the legs and the rails. In this table, slender legs (of the same width from midpoint to the frame) join the rails without any sense of integration,

FIG. 214 *Lady with a Harp: Eliza Eichel-berger Ridgely,* 1818, by Thomas Sully (1783-1872). Oil on canvas. Inscribed in lower left on harp "TS1818." National Gallery of Art, Washington, D.C., Gift of Maude Monell Vetleson.

FIG. 215 Card table, 1805-20, New York,
New York. Mahogany, mahogany veneer,
eastern white pine, black cherry, and tulip
poplar. Yale University Art Gallery, Mabel
Brady Garvan Collection.

FIG. 216 Painting on a wall in Pompeii,
Italy, prior to A.D. 79.

FIG. 216

FIG. 215

and the leaf-carved rectangles on the canted front corners seem to carefully separate the legs from the rails. It took time before I realized this is a wooden interpretation of an antique bronze table, an echo of a metal form that did not need to acknowledge the characteristics of wood. The Pompeian wall painting (figure 216) shows the type of object the New York table emulates.[4]

The richness of the New York table's veneers, including the cross-banded, half-round moldings on the edges of the top boards, the quality of the carved leafage, hairy legs, and paw feet, and the balance of parts, makes this a superb Greco-Roman statement. During the previous period, the upper leaf of a two-top table was supported when opened by a swing leg. During this period, as here, the lower leaf of a double top is usually bolted through a brace running from back to front within the frame so that both leaves can pivot on the bolt 90 degrees. When opened, both the upper and lower tops are supported by the frame. The frame has a bottom, and after pivoting the top and before opening the upper leaf, there is access to a storage area lined with green wool.

In 1845, the New York furniture maker and businessman Duncan Phyfe was one of the wealthiest people in New York. He was born in Scotland in about 1768 and moved to Albany, New York, in 1783 or 1784. In 1793, he was listed in the directories at 2 Broad Street in New York. In 1795, he was at 35 Partition Street (now Fuller Street, with the buildings numbered differently). He expanded to three buildings by 1811, and in 1817 he added a residence across the street. His first three buildings became shop, display room, and storage building.[5] When American furniture began to be collected late in the nineteenth century, Phyfe's earlier fame made his name synonymous with nearly all the furniture produced in New York from 1800 to 1825. Today, it is understood that he was one of the best known among many makers working in New York, and that on occasion, he bought furniture by other makers to sell in his shop.[6] Phyfe, as others, first produced neoclassical furniture with straight-turned legs, which are often reeded. By at least 1807, the same back could be purchased with straight, reeded legs or saber-shaped legs as in figure 217.[7] It continues to surprise just how many styles Phyfe produced, many of them at the same time. By the time he retired in 1847, you could have purchased from him during one visit at least four styles of furniture.

The side chair (figure 217) was made about 1805–20 by Duncan Phyfe for the home of the New Jersey governor, William Livingston. It is typical of the quality expected of his shop: the wood and the reeding on the sides expand as they move down from the top rail and along the top of the side seat rails; the recessed panels in the top rail and the upper halves of the front legs are patterned mahogany veneer set into solid mahogany; the hairy legs and paw feet are beautifully carved. Such chairs derive their shape from the Greek *klismos* form, best known from its depiction on Greek vases. The main lines curve up each side from the front feet to the seat rail, and from there they sweep through the seat rails to roll over at the top. To achieve this, a radically new concept of construction was developed. The basic form treats each side as one unit: front leg, seat rail, and back stile (which is one piece from the floor to the top). These side units are joined by four constructional rails: two seat rails that support an upholstered frame, and a lower and upper back rail. (In previous construction, the sides were not envisioned as a unit; rather, the vertical front legs and back stiles were joined by four seat rails; at the top, the back stiles were joined by a crest rail; the splat, or support for the sitter's back, ran vertically.) In the new construction, the two horizontal back rails hold fragile classical references such as a lyre, harp, or straight or curving crossed members. An additional horizontal rail can allow a more complex back as in figure 218.

While the name Phyfe too readily signals the neoclassical and Greco-Roman styles in New York, John and Thomas Seymour have incorrectly been associated with most of the blond, highly styled furniture produced in the Boston area. Only about six documented pieces by them are known. In 1785, John Seymour and his family moved from Devon, England, to Falmouth (now Portland), Maine. In 1794, the family moved to Boston, where John and his son Thomas worked together until Thomas left to set up his own warehouse in 1804. John ended his business in 1813 and Thomas continued on his own.[8] The few documented Seymour pieces are exquisitely crafted and feature the kinds of detailing found in Thomas Sheraton's published designs and those in *The London Chair-Makers' and Carvers' Book of Prices for Workmanship* of 1802 and its 1808 supplement.[9]

The Grecian form chair (figure 218) shows the quality of line and enrichment associated with the Seymours. The tablet in the top rail, the front faces of the large rectangle formed by the back stiles and two lower rails, and the upper part of the curved front legs are inlaid with flame-grained birch veneer; the visible parts of the seat rails are veneered with flaming birch. (On nearly identical chairs, the enrichment of the rectangle of the back and the seat rails use mahogany veneers and create a more forceful enclosing unit.) On figure 218, the ends of the top rail, the upper parts of the back stiles, and the bases of the front legs are reeded.

A designer's attempt to achieve a Greek flow of line was not always visually successful. The Greek form of sofa usually has four turned legs, or four bold C-shape legs that curve down and out from the ends of the seat rails; their simple lines play against the curves of the ends of the piece. In figure 194, the designer seems to have thought of two sets of chair legs as appropriate supports.

FIG. 217

FIG. 218

FIG. 217 Chair, 1805-20, New York, New York, by Duncan Phyfe (ca. 1768-1854). Mahogany and mahogany veneer. The Metropolitan Museum of Art, Gift of the Family of Mr. and Mrs. Andrew Varick Stout, in their memory, 1965 (65.188.2)

FIG. 218 Chair, 1805-20, Boston, Massachusetts. Mahogany, birch veneer, maple, and birch. Museum of Fine Arts, Boston, The M. and M. Karolik Collection of Eighteenth-Century American Arts.

FIG. 219 Chair, 1808-15, Boston, Massachusetts, by
Samuel Gragg (1772-1855). Ash and hickory; painted
yellow and red. Branded "S.GRAGG/BOSTON/PATENT."
Winterthur Museum.

FIG. 220 Chair, 1815-30, Baltimore, Maryland. Maple; painted yellow and red with stenciled and freehand gilt decoration. The Metropolitan Museum of Art, Purchase, Mrs. Paul Moore Gift, 1965 (65.167.6).

Samuel Gragg of Boston created the ultimate in unified lines when he used steam-bent laminated wood to produce figure 219. Each front leg, its side seat rail, and back side member is one unit. Windsor chair and hoop makers had long mastered steam bending; Gragg was a Windsor chair maker and his father a New Hampshire wheelwright. Gragg patented his "elastic chair" in August 1808 and advertised "Patent CHAIRS and SETTEES, with elastic backs and bottoms" the following May. He stayed in business until 1815.[10] The chair is painted what was called Pompeian red and yellow. The front seat rail and front stretcher use the colors to simulate reeding.

After 1805, the parts of the neoclassical style grew ever more massive (contrast figures 206 and 207), and, from about 1810, the Greco-Roman taste became ever more vigorous in line. The painted chair (figure 220) is based on Roman rather than Greek ideas, and severity is replaced by visual excitement. Gone are the flowing lines from front foot to top rail. Rather, the side seat rails have become major players in the design as they jut back past the supporting separate rear legs and curved back. Pompeian red and yellow freehand and stenciled decoration focuses and delineates the surfaces.

The French Connection

France had long been one of the sources for English designs. Chippendale called his upholstered chairs in the rococo style "French Chairs," and it is possible to trace French ideas into English neoclassical and Greco-Roman designs. After the American Revolution, the English taste in furniture continued to dominate American forms, but there was a strong influence of a rather different taste that came directly from France. The earlier French neoclassicism associated with Louis XVI (reign 1785–95) is related to the neoclassical style covered in Sections 22 and 23. Empire-style furniture associated with Napoleon, who crowned himself emperor in 1804, is more complex in form and more richly appointed, but underlying its elaborate surfaces are basic shapes that were appropriate for less grand members of French society. Many of these were embraced by some Americans. France had supported the American Revolution, and the activities of the marquis de Lafayette, who served in the Continental army from 1777 to 1781, made him a national hero.

After the Revolution, several French cabinetmakers moved to American style centers and produced furniture using France's simpler styling. One of the finest interpreters of the taste was Charles-Honoré Lannuier, who worked in France and then in New York, where he was first recorded in 1803, until his death in 1819.[1] In New York, he exploited his French training by advertising himself as a French *ébéniste*. Like other savvy cabinetmakers, he could, when asked, produce furniture in the English taste.[2] The Lannuier bedstead and card table (figures 221 and 222) are amongst his most elaborate pieces and as near French Empire taste as America achieved at this date. The bedstead was made for Harriet and Stephen Van Rensselaer. The form sat with the back of the long side pushed against the wall under drapery suspended from a central point, from which it flowed left and right to fall over the ends (as seen in the upper left corner of figure 241). Like the yellow chair (figure 220), part of the bed's excitement lies in the display of slightly disjunctive parts: the center section of the main rail is recessed, and its ends project as rectangular panels above *vert antique* and gilded dolphin feet. Above,

FIG. 221 Bedstead, 1817-19, New York, New York, by Charles-Honoré Lannuier (1779-1819). Mahogany, burl elm and rosewood veneers, maple, white pine, ash, and cherry; iron, gilded brass, die-stamped brass, gilded gesso, and *vert antique*. Two engraved labels. Albany Institute of History and Art, Gift of Constance Van Rensselaer Thayer (Mrs. William) Dexter.

FIG. 222 Card table, 1817, New York, New York, by
Charles-Honoré Lannuier (1779–1819). Mahogany
veneer, mahogany, tulip poplar, white pine, ash, and
basswood; iron, gilded brass, die-stamped brass, gilded
gesso, and *vert antique*. Inscribed in ink on brace
below top "Fait a New-York / Le I May 1817 / H"; in
ink on top of the figure's head "1817 / May / H." The
Metropolitan Museum of Art, Gift of Justine VR
Milliken, 1995 (1995.377.1).

bands with four stars are surmounted by richly decorated, separate curving pieces.

The movement of the card table is thrilling: inwardly thrusting two-colored legs support a multicurved mahogany-veneered plinth; a gilded figure leans forward to support the front edge of the frame; a pair of two-colored, leaf-enriched columns support the back edge. The brass detailing on such pieces was generally imported from France. Many pieces of the neoclassical and the Greco-Roman style are supported on casters. Often, particularly on small objects that were carried about—like sewing tables—and on large case pieces, the casters are visual terminals to the legs rather than functioning additions.

Although Lannuier did produce quieter pieces, the more contained side table in figure 223 was made in the French taste by the Boston firm of Thomas Emmons and George Archibald, who worked together from 1813 to 1825. It uses imported French mounts. Particular to Boston is the more compact stance and the flattened ball feet edged with brass trimming.

FIG. 223 Pier table, Boston, Massachusetts, by Thomas Emmons and George Archibald (working together 1813-25). Mahogany, mahogany veneer, chestnut, and pine, King of Prussia marble; gilded brass and silvered glass. Stenciled label of Emmons and Archibald on top of board under marble. Museum of Fine Arts, Boston, Gift of Mr. and Mrs. George C. Seybolt.

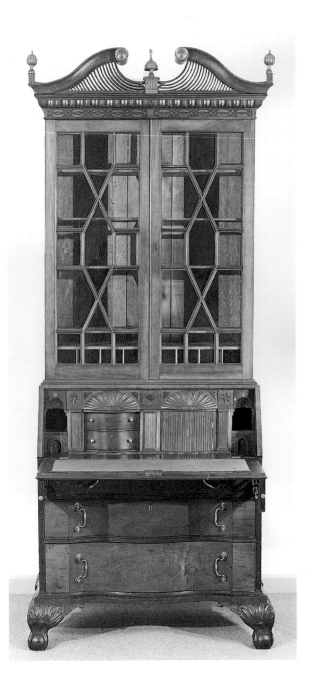

Rural Freedom

The visually powerful desk and bookcase (figure 224) was made by John Shearer in Martinsburg, Berkeley County, Virginia. He is thought to have emigrated with his parents from Edinburgh, Scotland, in 1775. The traditional elements—claw-and-ball feet; blocked shell-capped drawers in the interior of the desk section; fretwork on the architrave of the cornice—play against neoclassical elements: serpentine shapes on the large drawers (here they are flanked by broad flat areas); tambour doors covering the blocked interior drawers; pattern of the glazed doors; and egg-and-dart molding below the low-curving, open-pierced pediment. An additional note of excitement results from the vertical placement of the drawer pulls, which play against the inner line of the flat ends of the drawers.

The chest of drawers in figure 225 is inscribed in pencil across the inside of the back: "This Buro was made/In the Year of our Lord/1795/by/Bates How." The identity of the maker is not certain, but he may have been an eighteen-year-old from Canaan, Connecticut.[1] As with figure 224, the piece joins long-standing habits of construction with new ideas in a strongly personal manner. A traditional habit is seen in the jutting top. The shaping of the drawer fronts may express a neoclassical tendency to gentle down the projecting parts of blocking (as found on figure 155), or it may simply be a reverse use of the more urban serpentine shape. The use of three rather than the more traditional four drawers could be a way of adding neoclassicism's broad smoothness to the design, be a means to cut the cost of another drawer, or reflect the maker's or buyer's visual preference. The use of "rope"-carved, engaged quarter columns and base molding continues an earlier decorative idea (figure 174) in a more linear manner. The smallness of the claw-and-ball feet could be a personal choice, show the limited ability of the maker, or be a means of scaling the feet to the often smaller feet of the neoclassical style. The form of the imported brasses is the clearest link with urban classicism. The piece has great presence, as it dramatically contains on all four sides the open movement of the front facade.

FIG. 224 Desk, 1801, and bookcase, 1806, Martinsburg, Virginia (now West Virginia), by John Shearer. Black walnut, yellow pine, and tulip poplar. Twenty inscriptions throughout the piece with such phrases as "Made by me, John Shearer Septr. 1801 from Edinburgh 1775/Made in Martinsburgh." Museum of Early Southern Decorative Arts.

FIG. 225 Chest of drawers, 1795, northwestern Connecticut, by Bates How (b. 1776). American black cherry and eastern white pine. Inscribed in pencil on inside of back: "This Buro was made/In the Year of our Lord/1795/by/Bates How." Yale University Art Gallery, Mabel Brady Garvan Collection.

Rural Vernacular Neoclassicism

Neoclassicism's simple shapes and enjoyment of brightly painted surfaces made it a natural taste for inexpensive rural work. The resulting forms were so practical that many continued far into the next century. To look at contemporary folk painting is to see, as in a piece of furniture, how the juxtaposition of clearly defined parts can create a powerful statement.

Trained urban cabinetmakers would have condemned the pieces included in this and the previous section, just as academically trained painters, including John Vanderlyn, dismissed contemporary folk painters such as the now much appreciated portrait painter Ammi Phillips (1788–1865). He was born in Berkshire County, Massachusetts. His training is unknown, but it is surmised that Phillips based his manner of painting on the locally made portraits he saw as he traveled and worked in the western areas of Connecticut and Massachusetts, and several neighboring counties in upstate New York. His style of painting changed over the years, perhaps in part because he saw new ways rural artists were depicting their sitters. Like many folk works, Phillips's are about line and areas of color—skin, arms and chest, face, hair, garments, props—including furniture and the walls behind. In the painting of Paulina Dorr (figure 226), the areas are united by lines moving up the edges of the arms to the chest, neck, and head, which commands the top half of the painting. The chair used by Dorr is a "fancy chair" that was probably made locally and owned by the sitter or the family of the house Phillips was using as a studio. It speaks factual truth about the sitter's time and place. The boldly formed dressing table (figure 90) has the same kind of local honesty.

John Vanderlyn was born in Kingston, New York, studied briefly with Gilbert Stuart, and then in 1796 went to spend four years in Paris. Vanderlyn returned to New York City in 1801, but two years later he went to work in Paris and Rome. His ambition was to be known as a history painter, but he also made distinguished portraits.

FIG. 227

FIG. 226 *Portrait of Paulina Dorr*, probably 1814-15, Chatham Center, Columbia County, New York, attributed to Ammi Phillips (1788-1865). Oil on canvas. Abby Aldrich Rockefeller Folk Art Center, Williamsburg, Virginia.

FIG. 227 *Portrait of Robert R. Livingston*, 1804, by John Vanderlyn (1775-1852). Oil on canvas. The New-York Historical Society.

FIG. 228 Oval-top table, 1790–1810, New England. Maple and pine; original red paint under a later coat of gray. Private collection.

FIG. 229 Card table, 1790–1830, New England. Maple and pine; original red paint; originally had a round brass pull with one post. Private collection.

FIG. 230 Table, 1790–1840, New England, purchased in central New Hampshire. Maple and pine; original red paint; never had a drawer pull. Private collection.

FIG. 228

His study of Robert R. Livingston (figure 227), painted abroad in 1804, uses classical props including a Greek-style chair, which is intended to connote the intellectual and cultural sophistication of the sitter and to link him to ancient wisdom. Vanderlyn returned again to America in 1815, and in 1825 wrote to his nephew and namesake that the work of the rural portraitist Ammi Phillips was "cheap and slight." He dismissed people who commissioned Phillips as unable to tell good art from bad, while accusing them of being solely concerned with saving money.[1]

The oval-top table (figure 228) should be contrasted with the rectangular base oval-top table (figure 33), the thrusting-leg William and Mary–style tables (figures 72 to 75), and the fairly quiet turned-leg, turned-foot table (figure 35). The visual stance of figure 228 is different than those of the earlier tables: the openness of form and leanness of parts reflect rural neoclassical elegance, as found in the Ammi Phillips portrait.

The red-painted card table (figure 229) has a pine top on a maple frame. Probably the paint originally obscured the grain pattern of the drawer front. The drawer originally had a single circular brass pull. It is quiet in demeanor, and there is a nice scaling and balance of vertical and horizontal parts.

The red-painted pine and maple table (figure 230) is so generic it could, with different woods and perhaps proportions, be dated throughout the nineteenth century and made in a variety of regions.

FIG. 229

FIG. 230

199

FIG. 231 Chest over drawers, 1820, Pelham, Massachusetts, by Moses Davis. Tulip poplar; original green paint; original keyhole escutcheons, pulls replaced. Inscribed in chalk on bottom: "Made March 28th/1820/by Moses Davis." Old Sturbridge Village.

Similar pieces were made of cypress in Louisiana in the first third of the century[2]; related tables of yellow pine are documented in Georgia from 1840 to 1860[3]; walnut versions from Texas are dated as late as the end of the century.[4] What makes the New England version pleasing is its balance of parts and the interaction between the rectangular drawer front, placed high against the top, and the rectangle of the front rail. That the drawer never had a pull allows the echoes between the rectangles full rein.

The green-painted piece (figure 231) is inscribed in chalk on the bottom: "Made March 28th/1820/by Moses Davis," who was twenty years old. It continues a practical storage form of chest over drawers that began in the seventeenth century. The neoclassical elements are the tightness of the form, the use of oval escutcheons (the pulls are replacements), and the curves of the front feet and skirt rail that are cut from a single board and applied to the front. There are no similar end boards; there the sides are shaped at the bottom to form the feet.

FIG. 232

FIG. 233

When there are rockers on a chair, it is often a question of whether they were added after the chair was made—a change made to thousands of early chairs throughout the nineteenth century. We know that those on figure 232 were put there by the initial maker because they have the same paint history as the rest of the chair: red covered by blue and then gray. When it was fashionable to remove paint from furniture and varnish the result, a maple surface was more valuable than one with the grain pattern of birch. The outer face of the left front leg of figure 232 was, during that time, scraped of paint. Perhaps because the chair is of birch, the rest of the paint history remains intact. Tall, lean, and generic, the chair has a nice play of turned parts—including the arms—against the curving sawn rockers and bent slats. It is the kind of form that influenced Shaker designs.

During the nineteenth century, thousands of simple slat-back chairs were produced across America. The form of the finial and the use of maple suggest that the three-slat chair (figure 233) was made in central New Hampshire, where it was found.

FIG. 232 Rocking armchair, 1810-80, New England, purchased in central New Hampshire. Birch and ash; original red covered by blue, then gray paint; old splint seat. Private collection.

FIG. 233 Chair, 1820-1900, purchased in Sandwich, New Hampshire, probably made locally. Maple; original red paint; new splint seat. Private collection.

Classicism and the Shakers

Mother Ann Lee brought the Shaker faith to America from the Manchester area of northern England in 1774, and the group settled in upstate New York. Since her death in 1784, men and women have shared equally the leadership of the Believers. In 1789, members began to form communities in New England and upstate New York on land owned by those who had joined. By 1830 there were about five thousand members divided amongst nineteen substantial Shaker communities that stretched from Maine to Indiana and Kentucky.[1] Today, there are about ten Believers living in the Sabbathday Lake, Maine, community. The tenets of the faith have remained: celibacy, confession of sins to an Elder or Eldress, and community property.

There was a happy confluence in that, when hundreds of members were moving into new communities, the prevailing style in rural areas was vernacular neoclassicism, which the Shakers pushed to even greater simplicity. The lean forms were easy to reproduce in great numbers inexpensively: they used local woods painted the prevailing neoclassical colors of red, red-brown, orange, yellow, and blue. There were differences in the objects produced in the differing Shaker communities, since they, to some degree, reflected what was being made nearby, but the requirement by the leaders that all members have similar things produced to a considerable degree an overriding aesthetic unity. The case of drawers (figure 234) is one of the earliest Shaker pieces and is dated 1806 on the back. It comes from the New Lebanon, New York, community where the central leaders lived and from which authority flowed. The piece is a tight tall box fitted with drawers. There is no cornice molding. The only enrichments are the applied arched bracket base with a top edge molding, and the arrangements of the drawers and wooden pulls. The grid of six long drawers, and an echoing grid of six short ungraduated ones, was a practical decision, but, as in so much Shaker material, the practical provided an interesting visual experience. The placement of the short drawers over long drawers tightens the top, while producing a play between the turned knobs on the different-length drawers.

FIG. 234 Case of drawers, dated in paint on back "1806," New Lebanon, New York. Pine colored red; maple knobs. Hancock Shaker Village, Pittsfield, Massachusetts.

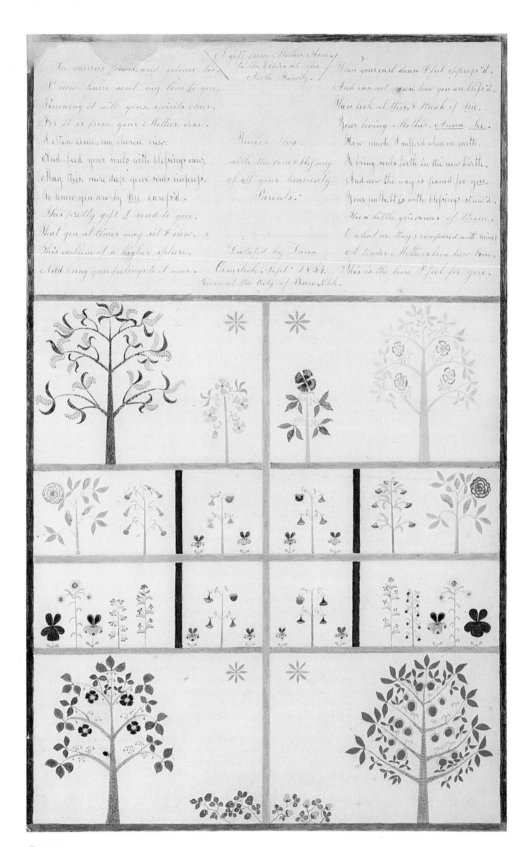

FIG. 235

Grids reflect neoclassicism's interest in order, and they and other organizing arrangements—squares, rectangles, circles, ovals, and linear designs—appear throughout Shaker communities. They were helpful when the task was to unite hundreds and then thousands of disparate Believers. The buildings in a community were arranged in grids and linear patterns, and such unifying patterns appear everywhere, including in Shaker textiles.

From 1837 to about 1850, there was such religious fervor among Believers that the communities were even more firmly closed against the influences of the outside world. Thus, while the world moved on to new styles, neoclassicism's contained forms and colors prevailed longer in Shaker hands. After about 1860, the Shakers were more involved with outsiders, and Shaker-made objects reflected again the styles prevailing outside their Shaker communities.

As part of the religious fervor, many members received gifts from the spirits of deceased Believers: songs, dances, and visions of the heaven they would occupy. Many of the latter were recorded on paper and are today called gift or spirit drawings. It is not surprising that some of them employ grids to reveal heavenly spaces and that they use the same pigments as found on Shaker furniture and woodwork. Figure 235 was drawn in the Hancock, Massachusetts, community in September of 1854, by Polly Collins. It is "A gift from Mother Ann. [Lee]/to the Elders at the/North Family." at Hancock. The expressed love of the grid in this drawing is like the rectangular patterns found on their furniture forms. The drawing takes a vertical sheet of paper and edges it with dark heavenly blue at the top and sides. The lower two-thirds is sequestered as a near-square with a bright green top and dark green bottom line. The near-square is divided into three tiers by a gray and a brown line; the central horizontal band is divided further into three squares by blue vertical lines. The near-square is also bisected by crossed yellow lines that create four large squares. All the small squares and rectangles thus formed on the near-square are filled with embroidery or appliqué-like trees and flowers. In another drawing, probably by Polly Collins, it is made clear that the lines dividing all these garden spaces are really narrow paths along which spirits can traverse: at all the junctions of the lines, there are small picket gates.

Many Shaker forms differ from similar non-Shaker pieces in how they include spaces and areas that suited a felt need—such as the small drawers in the top of figure 234—even when that produces a nontraditional rhythm of parts. The abrupt shift in the height of the drawers in figure 236 produces a delightful play between chest area, thin drawer, and deep drawers. The shield-shaped lock escutcheon pulls the eye upward. The dark hue of the yellow on such a formal piece, and the use of an ornamental escutcheon, indicates an early date. By the 1830s most objects were nearly as stringent as

FIG. 235 Gift drawing, 1854, Hancock, Massachusetts, by Polly Collins. Ink and watercolor on paper. Inscribed "A gift from Mother Ann./to the Elders at the/North Family… Sept 1854." Andrews Collection, Hancock Shaker Village, Pittsfield, Massachusetts.

FIG. 236 Chest over drawers, 1810-20, Watervliet or New Lebanon, New York. Pine, maple pulls; original yellow paint or stain, varnished; embossed tin lock escutcheon. Seattle Art Museum, acquired in honor of John T. Kirk. Purchased from the American Furniture Fund, Decorative Arts Acquisition Fund, and Margaret E. Fuller Purchase Fund.

the tall case of drawers in figure 234. The employment of a molding around three sides of the top, and a bracket base dovetailed at the front corners, suggests it originated in the Watervliet, New York, community. However, the small vertical breaks in the curve of the feet (as on figure 234) are normally associated with New Lebanon pieces.

The Shakers had strict rules about how to handle wooden pieces so they would be protected from wear until the end of the Millennium, which the Shakers believed had started when the Shaker faith began. One of the differences between Shaker and non-Shaker pieces is in their surfaces. Non-Shaker pieces often show the tool marks made during production, and extensive wear from use during the ensuing years. The Shaker pieces, which employ the same woods, were more smoothly finished before being painted as part of the Shakers' striving for perfection. Also, the Shakers' rules for careful use mean that pieces which remained in Shaker hands saw little surface wear. Today, Shaker collectors demand pristine surfaces and vivid paint, while those collecting rural, vernacular, non-Shaker forms demand signs of construction and use.[2]

Shaker oval boxes and oval carriers, made with the same construction, have long been valued by the Shakers and non-Shakers for their smooth, tight, oval patterns that seem to personify the Shakers' concern for careful, pristine pieces. Even when collectors, and the Shakers themselves, were stripping paint from Shaker furniture to make it part of the colonial revival's preference for natural woods, many people valued and left untouched these small painted forms. The mid-nineteenth-century yellow carrier from Canterbury, New

FIG. 237 Oval carrier, 1850-60, Canterbury, New Hampshire. Maple, pine, and ash; copper tacks; painted yellow. Collection of Dr. and Mrs. M. Stephen Miller.

Hampshire (figure 237), is typical of the tight forms, pristine surfaces, and brilliant colors that once dominated Shaker life.

From their earliest days, the Shakers have sold their chairs "into the world," to non-Shakers, as part of a community's products that provided income. The early chair (figure 238) was made in the Enfield, New Hampshire, community. When compared to the "worldly" chair of about the same date (figure 232), both show a vertical painted stance. The Shaker chair is new in its stringency of parts and communicates the care with which the Shakers use their domestic pieces. The rear legs are fitted with tilters: turned wooden balls with flat bases that fit into rounded hollows in the bases of the back posts. They are held in place by leather thongs. These protected the painted floors and carpets against wear when a sitter leaned backwards. The seat lists that hold the cane are surprisingly slender for a chair that anticipates a leaning sitter: they are only one inch from front to back at their center point, and, being flattened top and bottom, are only three-quarters of an inch vertically. They are also pierced with holes for the cane. Careful, conscious sitting was required.

As part of the Shakers' ordered existence, many rooms were numbered, and many of the pieces that were to exist in them for the Millennium have corresponding numbers. The back of the top splat of figure 238 is stenciled "12" in black paint, so it could always be returned to room 12.

As a means of generating income late in the nineteenth century, the South family at Mount Lebanon (the name had been changed from New Lebanon to Mount Lebanon in 1861) produced thousands of chairs and, with the aid of a catalogue, sold them widely. The products were numbered by size, and figure 239 shows some of the variations that the Shakers made available. Chairs with round-top rails, rather than finials, permitted the use of full-height back cushions, along with seat cushions, that the Shakers also produced (figure 240). Their red and black colors derive from the fashionable use of the colors of Asian lacquerware.

FIG. 238 Chair, 1840-60, Enfield, New Hampshire. Birch; painted red; cane seat. Back of top slat stenciled in black "12." Collection of Dr. and Mrs. M. Stephen Miller.

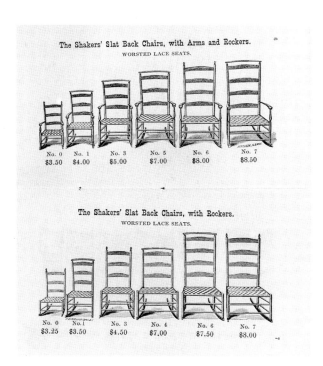

FIG. 239

FIG. 240

FIG. 239 Chair catalogue, about 1880, Mount Lebanon (name changed from New Lebanon to Mount Lebanon in 1861), New York. On cover "Illustrated Catalogue and Price List of Shakers' Chairs Manufactured by the Society of Shakers. R. M. Wagon & Co., Mount Lebanon, New York." Collection of the Shaker Museum and Library, Old Chatham, New York.

FIG. 240 Number 7 production rocking armchair, Mount Lebanon, New York. Chair purchased from the community on November 10, 1873. Maple; stained a dark mahogany color; cushions made for a number 6 chair; warp and weft: cotton or linen; pile: wool. Collection of the Shaker Museum and Library, Old Chatham, New York.

MODERN PRACTICES

American life changed dramatically in the nineteenth century as capitalism flourished. Cities grew rapidly as immigrants from the countryside and abroad swelled their populations. A wage-earning labor force emerged as factories overshadowed the family-centered artisan systems that had been in place since the early colonial period. From 1840, there was an ever greater use of machines to do what had been labor intensive: roller printing made wallpaper and textiles cheap; except in luxury situations, pressed glass replaced blown glass; water power turned lathes, planers, and mortising machines. New saws could cut more sheets of veneer from the same amount of wood. Jigsaws made complex shapes easy, and machines created low-relief carving.

Where before the richly appointed interior had a degree of simple clarity, in the new age most people at all levels of society could have a significant number of things. Walls and floors were covered, windows draped, and furniture moved out from the walls to be arranged around a center table lit by oil lamps and then gas chandeliers. Styles changed rapidly and overlapped each other for decades. Early and late versions of a style do differ significantly and can be dated accordingly, but the Greek and Gothic taste was in fashion from 1830 to 1875; the Elizabethan and rococo from 1830 to 1860; and the Renaissance, Egyptian, and other styles from 1860 to 1880. From the late nineteenth century, companies in Grand Rapids, Michigan, and other mass production firms produced elements of most of the styles, often combining several on the same piece.

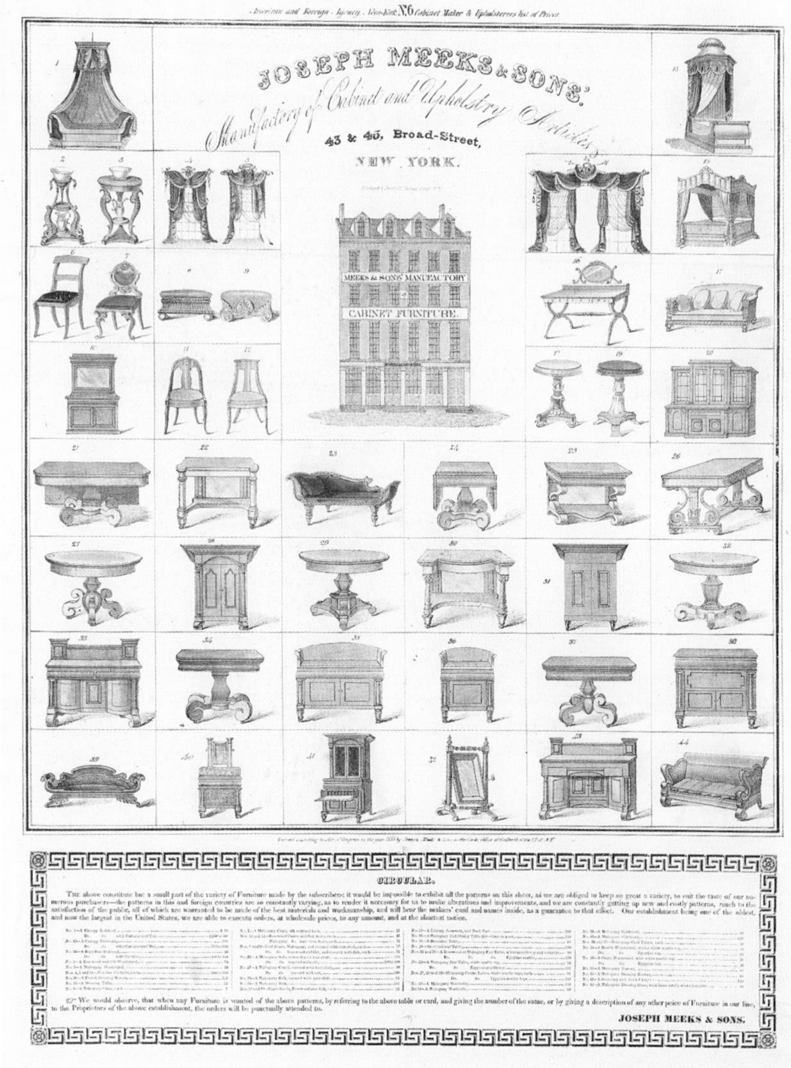

FIG. 241 Trade advertisement for Joseph Meeks & Sons', 1833, by George Endicott and Moses Swett, New York. Hand-colored lithograph. The Metropolitan Museum of Art, Gift of Mrs. R. W. Hyde, 1943 (43.15.8).

A Plethora of Styles and the Revival of American Designs

The Joseph Meeks and Sons' advertisement of 1833 (figure 241) demonstrates the beginnings of this plenitude: a French-style bed placed flat against the wall below centrally suspended drapery; complex curtains for windows; Greek and rococo revival chairs placed next to each other—one with a flat surface, one with carving. Most of the forms have flat, easy-to-produce surfaces enriched by patterned veneers. On similar, less expensive versions, the grain patterns were supplied by painted graining.

A look at the illustrated catalogue of London's "Great Exhibition," held at the Crystal Palace in 1851, is an opportunity to see the proliferation of stylistic quotations: Egyptian, Greek, Celtic, Gothic, Renaissance, Elizabethan, Louis XVI, rococo, and various hybrids. Although the "Great Exhibition" showed mostly expensive objects, some of the furniture styles were available inexpensively in painted wood, bentwood, cast iron, and pressed leather, which "possesses the tone and effect of wood-carving, at a considerable diminution of expense . . ."[1] A few American products were represented. Interspersed throughout this plenitude were modern carriages.

FIG. 242 Étagère, 1850-60, New York, New York, by Alexander Roux (ca. 1813-1886). Rosewood, chestnut, tulip poplar, and maple; silvered glass. The Metropolitan Museum of Art, Saysbury Mills Fund, 1971 (1971.219.220).

The midcentury étagère, by the French immigrant cabinetmaker Alexander Roux (figure 242), uses laminated rosewood to produce a frothy rococo revival form on which objets d'art could be displayed. On many less expensive rococo revival pieces, the best carving is on the upper part where it is readily seen, while lower areas received less attention.

Although from the second quarter of the nineteenth century various English designers, such as A.W.N. Pugin and John Ruskin, had worked against the machine aesthetic, it was at the end of the century that reformers established a beachhead against the flow of complexity. The late nineteenth-century arts and crafts movement sought to reestablish the role of the handmade, and was the first major movement to seek inspiration from the countryside. Where before styles had flowed out from urban areas and often became quite transformed by rural makers, the arts and crafts designers, in seeking honest workmanship and practical designs, sought inspiration from simple early country pieces. The first official arts and crafts organization in America was the Society of Arts and Crafts, Boston, created in 1897. Many designers worked in this style. After visiting Europe to observe various arts and crafts shops, Gustav Stickley (1857–1942) began his own Craftsman Workshops (1899–1916) in Eastwood, New York. Between 1901 and 1916, he published the magazine *The Craftsman,* which broadly popularized the look.

In his 1909 *Craftsman Homes,* Stickley brought together a range of designs he had previously published in *The Craftsman* magazine. The book includes metalwork, fabrics, needlework, and furniture—and how it should be finished—with an array of pleasant house designs that range from a small one of log construction to a larger home with a tower. The "Corner of the livingroom" in "A Bungalow of Irregular Form" (figure 243) is perhaps the book's most "early American" interior. It features an open raftered ceiling, bold fireplace, grids of square-paned glass in door and windows, window benches, and, as freestanding objects, a bookcase, table, and cushioned adjustable-back armchair. None of these features would have been present in this way in a living room prior to the overlaying of arts and crafts ideals with a colonial revival gloss.

FIG. 243 *A Bungalow of Irregular Form,* 1909. Print from Gustav Stickley, *Craftsman Homes,* p. 65. Courtesy, Stephen Gray.

FIG. 244 Bookcase, 1912-16, East-wood (Syracuse), New York, by Gustav Stickley's Craftsman Workshop. Oak; original dark finish. Cabinetmaker's compass and "Stickley" branded on left face of right rear leg, and Craftsman's paper label on underside of top shelf. Private collection.

The Gustav Stickley bookcase (figure 244) has both a large Crafts-man paper label and the brand of Stickley's workshop. The piece uses his favorite wood and silhouettes both the parts and the whole with a dark finish. The finish was accomplished by placing the piece in a tent with ammonia fumes, which reacted to the tannin in the wood. Then, with aniline stain, the color unified. Finally, it was shellacked and waxed.[2] Like the framed chests of the seventeenth century (figures 10 and 11), it is a play of verticals, horizontals, and panels. But the piece mixes formality and informality as it varies the thickness of the parts and allows air and light to pass through the members. It allies with the modernists' urge to fragment solid forms—as found in cubism and the styles it generated.

Concurrent with the rise of the arts and crafts impulse, and par-tially influenced by it, many Americans began to look at their own past and collect early American material. This naturally led to the reproduction of early pieces. The best known proponent was Wallace

Nutting, who developed a many-faceted business in Framingham,
Massachusetts. He wrote various books, and his 1928 two-volume
Furniture Treasury, with five thousand photographs, became the bible
for generations of furniture collectors and remains an important
source of images. His hand-tinted platinum prints of women in
colonial costume, doing domestic activities in authentic colonial
rooms with authentic furniture (mostly taken in the five museum
houses he owned), sold by the tens of thousands. He also repro-
duced early hardware. But he is most famous for his personal collection of early American furniture—purchased by J. P. Morgan
and given to the Wadsworth Atheneum in Hartford, Connecticut,
in 1925—and his reproduction of early American furniture forms.
It was Nutting's collection of American furniture that Armand
LaMontagne was visiting when he decided to make the fake chair
included here as figure 47, and get it into a major museum.

In 1917 Nutting began a furniture firm that produced Windsor

FIG. 246 Continuous-bow Windsor child's high chair, about 1930-40, Framingham, Massachusetts, by Wallace Nutting (1861-1941). Birch, oak, and white pine; surface purposefully aged. Appears as number 210 in *Wallace Nutting General Catalogue, Supreme Edition* (1930). Winterthur Museum.

chairs. By 1924 he was also making seventeenth-century forms; then eighteenth-century style furniture was added to the line.[3] Nutting felt free (as in figure 245) to exaggerate, to make what he considered to be the perfect example of a form should it ever be found. The chair relates most clearly to the early eighteenth-century chair (figure 68). But its parts have the scale of seventeenth-century turned chairs—bigger meant earlier, which meant better. Early banister-back chairs (figure 67) have the front stretchers used here. New England slat-backs gained a simple ring-and-baluster-shaped front stretcher only as the century progressed. The form of the slats is too tall, and the outline of the top one is not known on an American slat-back chair. All early New England slat-back chairs were painted, but the clean, varnished look took precedence over historical fact, of which Nutting was aware. The chair possesses the gusto of a delight in bold—meaning early—Americana. Nutting's mistake—if it was a mistake and not purposeful, like LaMontagne's when he altered reality to make a unique statement—was to exaggerate for effect.

The continuous-bow Windsor child's high chair (figure 246) was for many years proudly displayed as an early piece by the Winterthur

FIG. 247 Advertisement for Drexel furniture.
From *The American Home* (March 1961), page 13.

Museum. The seat has shrinkage cracks, and the light green paint shows wear. The opening of one of the stretcher-to-leg joints exposed round tenons that were too white to be early, and their form showed they were machine produced: the mortise was bored with a flat-end center bit rather than a round-nosed spoon bit. Nutting knew and reported in his furniture catalogue that his pieces were often aged and sold as old: "A child's high chair made by me, and sold as new for nineteen dollars, was artificially aged and resold for a cool thousand. Nobody but the maker could have discovered the imposition."[4]

The chair appears as figure 210 in a Nutting catalogue, where it is one of four Windsor-style children's high chairs, and they all look "wrong." None has a footrest. They are all very shiny and very pretty. Three use the long tapered base to the legs as found on figure 246. When this long, smooth taper is focused upon, it is clearly too smooth and long to be in scale with the ring, reel, and baluster forms at the top of the legs and under the ends of the arms. It looks as though it were extended by a computer manipulating a shorter leg design.

Even a gifted and trained modern eye can for a variety of reasons make mistakes. Many curators, collectors, and dealers found the child's high chair in figure 246 a truly beautiful eighteenth-century piece—even though a depiction of it appears in a Nutting catalogue. Perhaps, if the Nutting image was known, those at Winterthur thought their chair was Nutting's source for his reproductions. It is always easy with hindsight to see what one should have seen.

Nutting's let-the-wood-show attitude has persisted. It reached a high point when furniture manufacturing boomed after World War II, and linked with it was a new colonial craze inspired by such restorations as Colonial Williamsburg. "Williamsburg Blue" became one of the most popular decorating colors. The Drexel furniture company purchased the rights to the name "Wallace Nutting" in the 1940s, and the text of its 1961 advertisement (figure 247) reads: "Drexel has gone to the sources of these pieces—among them Wallace Nutting's 'Furniture Treasury', to bring you American Treasury, styled for our way of living today. The woods are rich and varied: figured cherry, maple clusters, knotty pine and sturdy pecan . . . all mellowed, with the look of years of hand care." The look fostered by the Drexel company now seems raw, but it was consistent with how real early furniture was being cleaned for use in homes and museums. It was this taste, which ruined thousands of pieces of early furniture, that caused me, and many others, to work to convince buyers to love the "ratty" during the 1960s and 1970s.

Conclusion

This book has had two themes: how cabinetmakers create beauty, and training the eye to understand the process. Every early American design with a pretension to style has its sources, no matter how much they have been reworked. The final statement is the maker's personal way of doing what was generally known in his region.

The joy of looking is to look with even greater appreciation and deeper understanding. To avoid mistakes, all kinds of scholarship need to be brought into play, but, finally, aesthetic enjoyment comes from seeing what is there.

Notes

Section 1

1. Charles F. Montgomery, then in charge of the collections at Winterthur Museum, flew his Winterthur students to see the exhibition in Hartford. Later he told me the show conditioned how he exhibited the Garvan and related collections at Yale University when he became their curator in 1970. At Yale, unlike at Winterthur, when he reinstalled the collection he made no reference to period arrangements but put pieces on pedestals and hung them on walls.

Section 2

1. For a brief discussion, see Bob Flexner, "Old Furniture Workshop; Warps: Their Causes and Cures," *Maine Antique Digest* (March 1999): 17–F. For more detailed discussions, see *Wood Handbook: Wood as an Engineering Material,* Agricultural Handbook, 72 (Washington, D.C.: Forest Products Laboratory, Forest Service, U.S. Department of Agriculture, 1974), section 4, 29–31; T. E. Timell, *Compression Wood in Gymnosperms* (Berlin, Heidelberg, New York, Tokyo: Springer-Verlag, 1986), 3:1801–24. I am grateful to Rock Hushka for bringing these books to my attention.

2. I recently straightened the bottom of a piece of sculpture made by Robert Morris in 1961. It consists of a cube about ten inches square made of walnut boards. The four sides are screwed together. The top and bottom boards are screwed to the top and bottom of the sides. The bottom board had warped, pulling with it some of the screws, and you could see into the cube. The bottom was removed and maple dowels used to plug the screw holes. This provided a firmer material for the replaced screws. I ironed the convex side of the bottom covered by canvas (which scorched) and took the board just slightly past straight. It was screwed in place and has remained straight.

Section 3

1. Before 1900, African material in its original state had been included in natural history museums. From about 1900, Pablo Picasso and other artists and collectors saw masks and figures stripped of paint, fur, cloth, raffia, and other attachments, and then polished, as parallel to cubism's emphasis on abstract forms. In 1914, Alfred Stieglitz created the first American show of African art in his New York Fifth Avenue gallery, where he juxtaposed mostly cleaned-up African pieces with avant-garde works from Europe. Although some untouched African artifacts were included in subsequent exhibitions, it was not until the 1972 Museum of Modern Art's "African Textiles and Decorative Arts" exhibition that a broad interest in accumulated surfaces and worn household objects became normal. In 1980, the traveling exhibition "African Furniture and Household Objects" further shifted the emphasis from the stripped to the complete. It was not until 1985 that fully costumed mannequins were exhibited. For further understanding of the issues involved, see Susan Vogel, "History of a Museum, with Theory," in *Exhibition*-ism: *Museums and African Art* (New York: Museum of African Art, 1994), 81–95. I am indebted to Pam McClusky for showing me the broad range of untouched African material owned by the Seattle Art Museum, discussing the history of the cleaned versus the untouched, and providing readings.

2. From 1965 to 1971 Danny Robbins, one of the people to whom this book is dedicated, was director of the Museum of Art, Rhode Island School of Design, in Providence, Rhode Island. In 1967, he brought to that museum from the Rose Art Gallery, Brandeis University, works that included this painting. I was then in charge of that museum's Pendleton Collection of spectacular American furniture.

Section 5

1. Sandpaper in Boston was discussed by Mack Headley in "Eighteenth-Century Cabinet Shops and the Furniture Making Trades in Colonial Newport," in papers presented at the conference on "New Perspectives on Rhode Island Furniture," held in New York, October 11–13, 1999.

Section 6

1. Benno M. Forman, *American Seating Furniture, 1630–1730: An Interpretive Catalogue* (New York and London: W.W. Norton, 1988), 28, 79.

Section 7

1. Philip Zea and Suzanne L. Flynt, *Hadley Chests* (Deerfield, Mass.: Pocumtuck Valley Memorial Association, 1992), 5. I am grateful to Philip Zea for providing further references and information about the Hadley group in February 1999.

The place of origin and date of about 1710 for figure 50 was provided by Zea in a letter to the owner, February 1999.

2. John T. Kirk, *American Furniture and the British Tradition to 1830* (New York: Alfred A. Knopf, 1982), 95–118.

Section 8
1. Philip Zea and Suzanne L. Flynt, *Hadley Chests* (Deerfield, Mass.: Pocumtuck Valley Memorial Association, 1992), 18–21.

2. Zea and Flynt, *Hadley Chests*, 22; I am grateful to Philip Zea and Susan Buck for writing to me about the chest's paint history in February 1999.

Section 9
1. I am indebted to Benno M. Forman for this information; for references to other high chests with related features, see Gerald W.R. Ward, *American Case Furniture in the Mabel Brady Garvan and Other Collections at Yale University* (New Haven: Yale University Art Gallery, 1988), 238.

2. Adam Bowett, "The English 'horsebone' Chair, 1685–1710," *The Burlington Magazine* 141, no. 1154 (May 1999): 269, 266.

3. For Boston, see Roger Gonzales and Daniel Putnam Brown, Jr., "Boston and New York Leather Chairs: A Reappraisal," in *American Furniture 1996*, ed. Luke Beckerdite (Milwaukee, Wis.: Chipstone Foundation, 1996), 188. For New York, see Neil D. Kamil, "Hidden in Plain Sight: Disappearance and Material Life in Colonial New York," in *American Furniture 1995*, ed. Luke Beckerdite and William N. Hosley (Milwaukee, Wis.: Chipstone Foundation, 1995), 213.

Section 10
1. Brock Jobe, "The Boston Furniture Industry, 1720–1740," in *Boston Furniture of the Eighteenth Century* (Boston: Colonial Society of Massachusetts, 1974), 42, 74.

2. Benno M. Forman, "Delaware Valley 'Crookt Foot' and Slat-Back Chairs: The Fussell-Savery Connection," *Winterthur Portfolio* 15, no.1 (Spring 1980): 41.

3. Robert Wemyss Symonds Papers, ms. 75 x 69.45, p. 49, Winterthur Library: Joseph Downs Collection of Manuscripts and Printed Ephemera.

Section 11
1. For example, the fronts of many six-board chests are painted, stamp-punched, carved, or decorated with applied moldings to make them appear as, or at least echo, the more expensive framed construction. See John T. Kirk, *Connecticut Furniture, Seventeenth and Eighteenth Centuries* (Hartford, Conn.: Wadsworth Atheneum, 1967), figs. 49, 32, 27, 26. A Middletown, Connecticut, desk and bookcase of 1760–90 has a pair of boards that cover the bookcase section. Each is carved to appear as though it consists of a panel held in a frame; with a great deal of labor, the maker carved into the solid deeply recessed grooves that make the doors appear like framed construction, as on figure 156. See the exhibition catalogue entitled *The Great River: Art & Society of the Connecticut Valley, 1635–1820* (Hartford, Conn.: Wadsworth Atheneum, 1985), 219.

2. Philip Zea and Suzanne L. Flynt, *Hadley Chests* (Deerfield, Mass.: Pocumtuck Valley Memorial Association, 1992), 10–11.

3. The edge moldings on two New York tea tables step down, rather than rising to act as a frame to keep items from slipping off an edge. The edges may have been recessed to hold the downwardly projecting edges of a silver or wooden tray. For the one with slightly simpler carving, see Joseph Downs, *American Furniture: Queen Anne and Chippendale Periods in the Henry Francis du Pont Winterthur Museum* (New York: Macmillan Co., 1952), fig. 374; for both the simpler and the table with slight additional carving, see Luke Beckerdite, ed., *American Furniture 1996* (Milwaukee, Wis.: Chipstone Foundation, 1996), 258–59. The latter appears with a later wooden tray in Luke Vincent Lockwood, *Colonial Furniture in America*, 3d ed. (New York: Charles Scribner's Sons, 1957), fig. 737.

4. Albert Sack, *The New Fine Points of Furniture: Early American* (New York: Crown Publishers, 1993), 264.

5. Morrison H. Heckscher, *American Furniture in the Metropolitan Museum of Art*, vol. 2, *Late Colonial Period: Queen Anne and Chippendale Styles* (New York: Metropolitan Museum of Art and Random House, 1985), 242–43.

6. John T. Kirk, *Early American Furniture* (New York: Alfred A. Knopf, 1970), 32.

7. It descended in the Sarah Bradlee Fulton (1740–1836) family. She was married in 1762 and lived in Boston. It was probably made for a member of the preceding generation.

8. Downs, *American Furniture*, fig. 186; Heckscher, *American Furniture*, 235.

9. William Macpherson Hornor, Jr., *Blue Book, Philadelphia Furniture: William Penn to George Washington* (1935; reprint, Washington, D.C.: Highland House Publishers, 1977), 207.

10. John T. Kirk, *American Furniture and the British Tradition to 1830* (New York: Alfred A. Knopf, 1982), 128–32.

11. John T. Kirk, *American Chairs, Queen Anne and Chippendale* (New York: Alfred A. Knopf, 1972), 183, fig. 244.

12. Kirk, *American Furniture and the British Tradition*, 240, fig. 783.

13. Benno M. Forman, "Delaware Valley 'Crookt Foot' and Slat-Back Chairs: The Fussell-Savery Connection," *Winterthur Portfolio* 15, no. 1 (Spring 1980): 44.

14. Kirk, *American Furniture and the British Tradition*, 240, fig. 782; 367, fig. 1471.

15. Forman, "Delaware Valley 'Crookt Foot,'" 63.

16. Benno M. Forman, "The Crown and York Chairs of Coastal Connecticut and the Work of the Durands of Milford," *Antiques* 105, no. 5 (May 1974): 1147–54.

Section 12
1. For Boston, see Leigh Keno, Joan Barzilay Freund, and Alan Miller, "The Very Pink of the Mode: Boston Georgian Chairs, Their Export, and Their Influence," in *American Furniture 1996*, ed. Luke Beckerdite (Milwaukee, Wis.: Chipstone

Foundation, 1996), 266–306. For a study of the economic problems and movement of artisans into and out of Boston from 1690 to 1760, see Robert Blair St. George, *Conversing by Signs* (Chapel Hill and London: University of North Carolina Press, 1998), 208–41. Newport's growth was discussed by Thomas S. Michie in "Shops, Houses, Wharves: Rhode Island Decorative Arts in Context, 1720–1820," and Phil Zea presented figures on vessels in "Commodious by Design: The Serpentine Furniture of Newport, Rhode Island," in papers presented at the conference on "New Perspectives on Rhode Island Furniture," held in New York, October 11–13, 1999.

2. William Rieder, "Eighteenth-Century Chairs in the Untermyer Collection," *Apollo* 107, no. 193 (March 1973): 183; C. Truesdell, "A Puzzle Divided: English and Continental Chairs Following a Unique Design of the Early Eighteenth Century," *Furniture History* 20 (1984): 57–60, pls. 76, 77, 78a, 78b.

3. Morrison H. Heckscher, "Copley's Picture Frames," in Carrie Rebora et al., *John Singleton Copley in America* (New York: Metropolitan Museum of Art, 1995), 142–59; Alan Miller, "Roman Gusto in New England: An Eighteenth-Century Boston Furniture Designer and His Shop," in *American Furniture 1993,* ed. Luke Beckerdite (Milwaukee, Wis.: Chipstone Foundation, 1993), 160–200.

4. Conversation between the author and Bill Stahl, July 19, 1999.

Section 13

1. Albert Sack discussed with the author Lansdell Christie's decision to gild his high chest's finials. The piece without gilded finials appears in James Biddle, *American Art from American Collections* (New York: Metropolitan Museum of Art, 1963), 29.

Section 14

1. Solomon Fussell's use of stain on Philadelphia maple chairs is cited in Section 11, note 13. For Job Townsend, see Martha Willoughby, "The Accounts of Job Townsend, Jr.," in *American Furniture 1999,* ed. Luke Beckerdite (Milwaukee, Wis.: Chipstone Foundation, 1999), 109–61.

2. I am grateful to Robert Mussey for providing this information during a conversation in July 1999.

3. In July 1999, Lance Mayer discussed his understanding that before the neoclassical period maple was first colored to resemble walnut and then mahogany. He provided further information on stains and paints; a photocopy of the relevant section of Robert Dossie's *The Handmaid to the Arts,* noting that the cabinetmaker Capt. Abel Spicer of Groton (now Ledyard), Connecticut, owned a copy; and corrected this part of the manuscript.

4. Robert Mussey reminded me of Dunlap's recipe for the stain, which is given in full in the exhibition catalogue prepared by Charles S. Parsons and entitled *The Dunlaps & Their Furniture* (Manchester, N.H: Currier Gallery of Art, 1970), 57.

5. For a Connecticut Chippendale high chest of drawers with maple legs that were stained to match its cherry case, see Gerald W. R. Ward, *American Case Furniture in the Mabel Brady Garvan and Other Collections at Yale University* (New Haven: Yale University Art Gallery, 1988), fig. 143.

6. See Gerald W. R. Ward, ed., *American Furniture with Related Decorative Arts, 1660–1830: The Milwaukee Art Museum and the Layton Art Collection* (New York: Hudson Hills Press, 1991), 128.

7. Susan Buck, in a letter to the author, June 1999, cautions that much of the dark finish on maple is "likely many accumulated layers of degraded finish, grime, and oil-dressings. These types of materials can turn almost black over time."

Section 15

1. Graham Hood, *American Silver: A History of Style, 1650–1900* (New York, Washington, and London: Praeger Publishers, 1971), 127.

Section 16

1. Martin Eli Weil, "A Cabinetmaker's Price Book," in Ian M. G. Quimby, ed., *American Furniture and Its Makers: Winterthur Portfolio 13* (Chicago and London: University of Chicago Press, 1971), 175–92.

2. I am grateful to Jack Lindsey for informing me about the uncertainty as to who produced the drawings.

Section 17

1. For a study showing about 1,500 pieces of British furniture that are closely related to American pieces, see John T. Kirk, *American Furniture and the British Tradition to 1830* (New York: Alfred A. Knopf, 1982).

Section 18

1. Chandeliers were still a very rare item at this date, and this room probably did not have one. Candles were expensive (those less well off could buy used candles), and paintings and inventories establish that when not in use chandeliers were empty—having been cleaned of dripping wax—and candle holders were in the kitchen until brought out for use. Certainly, the modern practice of burning a quarter inch of new candles, to suggest they are not new, would not have been understood at this time. If there were a carpet, it would have been earlier and smaller.

2. Helena Hayward, ed., *World Furniture: An Illustrated History* (New York and Toronto: McGraw-Hill Book Co., 1965), 152, fig. 560.

3. Morrison H. Heckscher, *American Furniture in the Metropolitan Museum of Art,* vol. 2, *Late Colonial Period: The Queen Anne and Chippendale Styles* (New York: Metropolitan Museum of Art and Random House, 1985), 283.

4. John T. Kirk, *Early American Furniture* (New York: Alfred A. Knopf, 1970), 17–18 (high style); 45 (scorched).

5. Wendy A. Cooper and Tara L. Gleason, "A Different Rhode Island Block-and-Shell Story: Providence, Provenance and Pitch-Pediments," in *American Furniture 1999,* ed.

Luke Beckerdite (Milwaukee, Wis.: Chipstone Foundation, 1999), 266–306.

6. I am grateful to John Bivins for discussing the use of the blocked form in the South, October 1999.

7. John T. Kirk, *American Furniture and the British Tradition to 1830* (New York: Alfred A. Knopf, 1982), 125–27.

8. Kirk, *American Furniture and the British Tradition*, 122.

9. The feet of the stand on a writing-desk-on-stand in the Minneapolis Institute of Arts (acc. no. 95.57) made in India (Vizaqapatam), 1725–35, for the British East India Company for use by an English customer in India or for export to Europe.

10. Kirk, *American Furniture and the British Tradition*, 120; Robert Hatfield Ellsworth, *Essence of Style: Chinese Furniture of the Late Ming and Early Qing Dynasties* (San Francisco: Asian Art Museum of San Francisco, 1998), 61.

11. Kirk, *American Furniture and the British Tradition*, 194–95.

Section 19
1. William Macpherson Hornor, *Blue Book, Philadelphia Furniture: William Penn to George Washington* (1935; reprint, Washington, D.C.: Highland House Publishers, 1977), 100.

2. Hornor, *Blue Book*, frontispiece and 101. The architrave has on it a later brass plaque that reads: "Owned by Jos. Wharton/of Walnut Grove–/Born in Phila.–Aug. 4, 1707/Died July 27, 1779."

3. I am grateful to Tom Kugelman for providing this information during a conversation and through letters in September and October 1999.

4. The authenticity of figure 181 has been questioned. I have long believed it to be original: when inspected closely it has the aesthetic and physical qualities of age. I am grateful to Tom Denenberg for looking at it and discussing it in detail, and for providing new photographs. Wendy Cooper studied the cartouche on figure 176, provided photographs, and discussed its characteristics. There is no reason to doubt the originality of either cartouche.

5. Patricia E. Kane, *300 Years of American Seating Furniture: Chairs and Beds from the Mabel Brady Garvan and Other Collections at Yale University* (Boston: New York Graphic Society, 1976), 140.

6. See the exhibition catalogue, *The Great River: Art & Society of the Connecticut Valley, 1635–1820* (Hartford, Conn.: Wadsworth Atheneum, 1985), 229.

Section 20
1. I am grateful to Karen Keane for this information. The auction was at Robert W. Skinner, Inc., Bolton, Massachusetts.

Section 21
1. Conversation between the author and Ralph Carpenter in May 1999.

2. *Christie's Magazine* (July/August 1999): 93.

3. Conversation between the author and Albert Sack in May 1999.

4. I am grateful to Lisa Becker for establishing the date in a letter to the author, July 27, 1999.

5. I am indebted for this discussion of the development of auction house prominence, and the sale of the first $100,000 pieces to conversations in May and June 1999, with Albert Sack, Dean Failey, and Leslie Keno. Bill Stahl answered a series of questions about the history of the $100,000 breakthroughs and spoke about arranging private sales between sellers and buyers, in July 1999.

6. Lita Solis-Cohen, "Sotheby's, New York City Winter Americana Auction," *Maine Antique Digest* (March 1999): 30–E.

7. For companion chest-on-chest and kneehole dressing table, see David B. Warren, *American Furniture, Paintings and Silver from the Bayou Bend Collection* (Houston: Museum of Fine Arts, 1975), figs. 121, 130. For the variety of names, see John T. Kirk, *American Furniture and the British Tradition to 1830* (New York: Alfred A. Knopf, 1982), 189.

8. Conversation between the author and Albert Sack in May 1999; the agent bidding was Harold Sack. The piece was purchased by Robert M. Bass.

9. I am grateful to Leslie Keno for discussing his looking at the piece in Paris and describing the construction of the bracket feet during a conversation in June 1999.

Two Phases of the Federal Period
1. Charles F. Montgomery, *American Furniture: The Federal Period in the Henry Francis du Pont Winterthur Museum* (New York: Viking Press, 1966), 10.

2. William H. Pierson, Jr., *American Buildings and Their Architects* (Garden City, N.Y.: Doubleday, 1976), 112.

3. Pierson, *American Buildings*, 61; John Summerson, *Architecture in Britain 1530 to 1830*, 5th ed. (Baltimore, Md.: Penguin Books, 1969), 111–18, 317–19.

Section 22
1. For the Philadelphia house, see Beatrice B. Garvan, *Federal Philadelphia, 1785–1825: The Athens of the Western World* (Philadelphia: Philadelphia Museum of Art, 1987), 37–38. For the Otis house, see the exhibition catalogue entitled *Paul Revere's Boston: 1735–1818* (Boston: Museum of Fine Arts, Boston, 1975), 155.

Section 23
1. J. Michael Flanigan, *American Furniture from the Kaufman Collection* (Washington, D.C.: National Gallery of Art, 1986), 110.

2. Patricia E. Kane, *300 Years of American Seating Furniture: Chairs and Beds from the Mabel Brady Garvan and Other Collections at Yale University* (Boston: New York Graphic Society, 1976), 212.

3. Nancy Goyne Evans, *American Windsor Chairs* (New York: Hudson Hills Press, 1996), 678 (quotation); 346, 386, 389, 390, 405, 520, 678 (basswood), 405 (molding).

Section 24
1. Conversation between the author and Gerry Ward in June 1999.

Section 25

1. For a longer discussion with more images, see John T. Kirk, *American Furniture and the British Tradition to 1830* (New York: Alfred A. Knopf, 1982), 31–43.

Section 26

1. Geoffrey Squire, *Dress and Society 1560–1970* (New York: Viking Press, 1974), 135.

2. Alice Morse Earle, *Two Centuries of Costume in America 1620–1820* (1903; reprint, Rutland, Vt.: Charles E. Tuttle, 1971), 2:768.

3. Squire, *Dress and Society*, 133.

4. For possible printed sources, see David L. Barquist, *American Tables and Looking Glasses in the Mabel Brady Garvan and Other Collections at Yale University* (New Haven: Yale University Art Gallery, 1992), 222.

5. Morrison H. Heckscher, "Duncan Phyfe, revisitus," *Antiques* 151, no. 1 (January 1997): 236–39.

6. Peter M. Kenny, Frances M. Bretter, and Ulrich Leben, *Honoré Lannuier, Cabinetmaker from Paris: The Life and Work of a French Ébéniste in New York* (New York: Metropolitan Museum of Art, 1998), 45.

7. Charles F. Montgomery, *American Furniture: The Federal Period in the Henry Francis du Pont Winterthur Museum* (New York: Viking Press, 1966), 120–21.

8. J. Michael Flanigan, *American Furniture from the Kaufman Collection* (Washington, D.C.: National Gallery of Art, 1986), 178.

9. Patricia E. Kane, *300 Years of American Seating Furniture: Chairs and Beds from the Mabel Brady Garvan and Other Collections at Yale University* (Boston: New York Graphic Society, 1976), 174.

10. Wendy A. Cooper, *Classical Taste in America: 1800–1840* (New York: Baltimore Museum of Art and Abbeville Press, 1993), III.

Section 27

1. Peter M. Kenny, Frances M. Bretter, and Ulrich Leben, *Honoré Lannuier, Cabinetmaker from Paris: The Life and Work of a French Ébéniste in New York* (New York: Metropolitan Museum of Art, 1998), 8, 32–33, 61, 98.

2. Kenny, *Honoré Lannuier*, 76, pl. 32.

Section 28

1. Gerald W. R. Ward, *American Case Furniture in the Mabel Brady Garvan and Other Collections at Yale University* (New Haven: Yale University Art Gallery, 1988), 143.

Section 29

1. Barbara C. and Lawrence B. Holdridge, *Ammi Phillips: Portrait Painter 1788–1865* (New York: Clarkson N. Potter, Inc., 1969), 14.

2. Jessie J. Poesch, *Early Furniture of Louisiana* (New Orleans: Louisiana State Museum, 1972), 71.

3. See the catalogue for an exhibition entitled *Neat Pieces, The Plain-Style Furniture of Nineteenth-Century Georgia* (Atlanta: Atlanta Historical Society, 1983), 96.

4. Lonn Taylor and David B. Warren, *Texas Furniture, The Cabinetmakers and Their Work, 1840–1880* (Austin and London: University of Texas Press, 1975), 186, 192, 194–95, 197, 199.

Section 30

1. For a full discussion of Shaker history, Shaker artifacts, and the non-Shaker influences on Shaker design, see John T. Kirk, *The Shaker World: Art, Life, Belief* (New York: Harry N. Abrams, 1997).

2. For a history of collecting Shaker materials and a contrast between collecting Shaker and non-Shaker objects, see Kirk, *Shaker World*, 127–29, 231–43.

Section 31

1. *The Industry of All Nations, 1851* (1851; reprint, New York: Crown Publishers, 1970), 33.

2. I am indebted to Mike Whitt for this information.

3. I am grateful to Tom Denenberg for reading the part on Wallace Nutting and making corrections and additions.

4. Wallace Nutting, *Wallace Nutting General Catalogue, Supreme Edition* (1930; reprint, Exton, Pa.: Schiffer Publications, 1977), 4.

Bibliography

The best recent series of articles on American furniture appears in an annual publication entitled *American Furniture*, edited by Luke Beckerdite, published by the Chipstone Foundation, Milwaukee, Wisconsin, and distributed by the University Press of New England since 1993. (In 1995 William N. Hosley co-edited the publication.) In the following bibliography, references to articles in this journal include only the title and year of publication (e.g., *American Furniture 1993*), as well as the relevant page numbers.

The information in *American Furniture* is "cutting edge," and the photographs are unusually clear. The authors employ a traditional art-history approach, discussing written documentations and comparative examples of American furniture and architectural details. The articles would benefit from a greater use of other contemporary American arts and related European examples. In attempting to establish more accurate dating for the pieces, the contributors often push them to the beginning of their style. This can cause a strange anomaly, when, for example, William and Mary pieces are dated 1700 to 1720 and Queen Anne forms 1730 to 1740 or 1750. This suggests nothing was produced between 1720 and 1730. Nonetheless, the articles should not be missed. Each issue contains a list of recent publications on American furniture compiled by Gerald W. R. Ward.

The following selective bibliography contains some of the publications that further the discussions in this volume. For a more extensive guide to sources, see Kenneth L. Ames and Gerald W. R. Ward, eds., *Decorative Arts and Household Furnishings in America, 1650–1920: An Annotated Bibliography* (Winterthur, Del.: Henry Francis du Pont Winterthur Museum, 1989), distributed by the University Press of Virginia, Charlottesville.

General

Woods and construction

Peter Follansbee and John D. Alexander. "Seventeenth-Century Joinery from Braintree, Massachusetts: The Savell Shop Tradition." In *American Furniture 1996*, 81–104.

R. Bruce Hoadley. *Understanding Wood: A Craftsman's Guide to Wood Technology*. Newtown, Conn.: Taunton Press, 1980.

Charles F. Hummel. *With Hammer in Hand: The Dominy Craftsmen of East Hampton, New York*. Charlottesville: University Press of Virginia for the Henry Francis du Pont Winterthur Museum, 1968.

Finishes: Analysis of paint and varnish

Paint: Susan Buck. "A Masonic Master's Chair Revealed." In *American Furniture 1994*, 162–72.

Varnish: Gregory Landrey. "The Conservator as Curator: Combining Scientific Analysis and Traditional Connoisseurship." In *American Furniture 1993*, 147–59.

Upholstery

Edward S. Cooke, Jr., ed. *Upholstery in America and Europe from the Seventeenth Century to World War I*. New York and London: W. W. Norton, 1987.

Leroy Graves and F. Carey Howlett. "Leather Bottoms, Satin Haircloth, and Spanish Beard: Conserving Virginia Upholstered Seating Furniture." In *American Furniture 1997*, 266–97.

Windsors

Nancy Goyne Evans. *American Windsor Chairs*. New York: Hudson Hills Press, 1996. While this book is packed with information, including early quotations, the captions, and generally the text, do not give the finish on the chairs illustrated.

Charles Santore. *The Windsor Style in America*. 2 vols. Philadelphia: Running Press, 1981, 1987. Provides less information than Evans, but the text is easier to read and the present surfaces are noted.

Shaker

John T. Kirk. *The Shaker World: Art, Life, Belief*. New York: Harry N. Abrams, 1997. Places Shaker objects in the context of Shaker history and non-Shaker artifacts. It reveals the dependence and independence of Shaker work.

Charles R. Muller and Timothy D. Rieman. *The Shaker Chair*. Canal Winchester, Ohio: Canal Press, 1984.

Timothy D. Rieman and Jean M. Burks. *The Complete Book of Shaker Furniture*. New York: Harry N. Abrams, 1993. Divides Shaker furniture by communities.

Relationships of British and American furniture

John T. Kirk. *American Furniture and the British Tradition to 1830.* New York: Alfred A. Knopf, 1982. Publishes 1,500 pieces of British furniture that are close to American work in construction practices, motifs, and forms; shows by comparison America's contribution to furniture history.

Silver

Graham Hood. *American Silver: A History of Style, 1650–1900.* New York, Washington, and London: Praeger Publishers, 1971.

Regions

New England

Brock Jobe and Myrna Kaye, with the assistance of Philip Zea. *New England Furniture, The Colonial Era: Selections from the Society for the Preservation of New England Antiquities.* Boston: Houghton Mifflin Co., 1984.

Nancy E. Richards and Nancy Goyne Evans, with Wendy A. Cooper and Michael S. Podmaniczky. *New England Furniture at Winterthur: Queen Anne and Chippendale Periods.* Winterthur, Del.: Winterthur Museum, 1997. Distributed by University Press of New England, Hanover and London. The quality of the illustrations is poor and the writing dense, but the information is thorough.

Connecticut

The Great River: Art & Society of the Connecticut Valley, 1635–1820. Hartford, Conn.: Wadsworth Atheneum, 1985.

Rhode Island

American Furniture 1999. The entire issue is devoted to Rhode Island furniture.

Margaretta M. Lovell. "'Such Furniture as Will Be Most Profitable': The Business of Cabinetmaking in Eighteenth-Century Newport." *Winterthur Portfolio* 26, no. 1 (Spring 1991): 27–62.

Philadelphia and Pennsylvania

Jack L. Lindsey et al. *Worldly Goods: The Arts of Early Pennsylvania, 1680–1758.* Philadelphia: Philadelphia Museum of Art, 1999.

Philadelphia: Three Centuries of American Art. Philadelphia: Philadelphia Museum of Art, 1976.

Southern

American Furniture 1997. The entire issue is devoted to articles about Southern furniture from seventeenth-century to neoclassical forms.

Wallace B. Gusler. *Furniture of Williamsburg and Eastern Virginia, 1710–1790.* Richmond: Virginia Museum, 1979.

Ronald L. Hurst and Jonathan Prown. *Southern Furniture, 1680–1830: The Colonial Williamsburg Collection.* Williamsburg, Va.: Colonial Williamsburg Foundation, in association with Harry N. Abrams, 1997.

Styles

Seventeenth-Century

Jonathan L. Fairbanks and Robert F. Trent. *New England Begins: The Seventeenth Century.* 3 vols. Boston: Museum of Fine Arts, Boston, 1982.

Robert Blair St. George. *The Wrought Covenant: Source Material for the Study of Craftsmen and Community in Southeastern New England, 1620–1700.* Brockton, Mass.: Brockton Art Center/Fuller Memorial, 1979.

Philip Zea and Suzanne L. Flynt. *Hadley Chests.* Deerfield, Mass.: Pocumtuck Valley Memorial Association, 1992.

Seventeenth-Century and William and Mary

Benno M. Forman. *American Seating Furniture, 1630–1730: An Interpretive Catalogue.* New York and London: W. W. Norton, 1988. Dense reading, but packed with information.

William and Mary

Roger Gonzales and Daniel Putnam Brown, Jr. "Boston and New York Leather Chairs: A Reappraisal." In *American Furniture 1996*, 175–94.

Neil D. Kamil. "Hidden in Plain Sight: Disappearance and Material Life in Colonial New York." In *American Furniture 1995*, 191–249.

Queen Anne

Joan Barzilay Freund and Leigh Keno. "The Making and Marketing of Boston Seating Furniture in the Late Baroque Style." In *American Furniture 1998*, 1–40.

Leigh Keno, Joan Barzilay Freund, and Alan Miller. "The Very Pink of the Mode: Boston Georgian Chairs, Their Export, and Their Influence." In *American Furniture 1996*, 266–306.

Queen Anne and Chippendale

Morrison H. Heckscher. *American Furniture in the Metropolitan Museum of Art.* Vol. 2, *Late Colonial Period: The Queen Anne and Chippendale Styles.* New York: Metropolitan Museum of Art and Random House, 1985.

Chippendale

Luke Beckerdite. "Immigrant Carvers and the Development of the Rococo Style in New York." In *American Furniture 1996*, 233–65.

Luke Beckerdite. "Origins of the Rococo Style in New York Furniture and Interior Architecture." In *American Furniture 1993*, 15–37.

Morrison H. Heckscher and Leslie Green Bowman. *American Rococo, 1750–1775: Elegance in Ornament.* New York and Los Angeles: Metropolitan Museum of Art and Los Angeles County Museum of Art, 1992. Distributed by Harry N. Abrams, New York.

Robert Mussey and Anne Rogers Haley. "John Cogswell and Boston Bombé Furniture: Thirty-Five Years of Revolution in Politics and Design." In *American Furniture 1994*, 73–105.

Federal

Wendy A. Cooper. *Classical Taste in America: 1800–1840.* New York: Baltimore Museum of Art and Abbeville Press, 1993.

William Voss Elder III. *Baltimore Painted Furniture: 1800–1840.* Baltimore: Baltimore Museum of Art, 1972.

Beatrice B. Garvan. *Federal Philadelphia, 1785–1825: The Athens of the Western World.* Philadelphia: Philadelphia Museum of Art, 1987. Distributed by the University of Pennsylvania Press.

Brock Jobe and Clark Pearce. "Sophistication in Rural Massachusetts: The Inlaid Cherry Furniture of Nathan Lombard." In *American Furniture 1998,* 164–96. A close look at rural ways of handling neoclassical forms.

Peter M. Kenny, Frances M. Bretter, and Ulrich Leben. *Honoré Lannuier, Cabinetmaker from Paris: The Life and Work of a French Ébéniste in New York.* New York: Metropolitan Museum of Art, 1998. Distributed by Harry N. Abrams, Inc., New York.

Charles F. Montgomery. *American Furniture: The Federal Period in the Henry Francis du Pont Winterthur Museum.* New York: Viking Press, 1966.

Deborah Dependahl Waters. "Is it Phyfe?" In *American Furniture 1996,* 63–80.

1830 to 1920

Anna Tobin D'Ambrosio, ed. *Masterpieces of American Furniture from the Munson-Williams-Proctor Institute.* Utica, N.Y.: Munson-Williams-Proctor Institute, 1999.

Wendy A. Kaplan et al. *"The Art That Is Life": The Arts and Crafts Movement in America, 1875–1920.* Boston: Museum of Fine Arts, 1987.

Donald C. Peirce. *Art & Enterprise: American Decorative Art, 1825–1917: The Virginia Carroll Crawford Collection.* Atlanta: High Museum of Art, 1999. Distributed by Antique Collectors' Club Ltd.

Index

Numbers in **bold** type refer to figure numbers.

PHOTOGRAPHIC CREDITS

Courtesy, Bruce Alexander Photography, Strawbery Banke Museum: fig. 207;
Harry Bartlett: fig. 23; E. Irving Blomstrann: figs. 104, 156, 163, 181, 245; Del
Bogart: fig. 110; Edward A. Bourdon: fig. 66; Richard Cheek: figs. 33, 125;
Michael Fredericks: figs. 27–32, 34–35, 37, 40, 50–51, 54, 234, 237–40; Erik
Gould: fig. 71; Nancy Green Photographers: fig. 48; Herndon Associates: fig. 70;
John T. Kirk: figs. 113, 186, 199, 208–13, 216; Paul Macapia: figs. 19–21, 36,
236, 244, 247; John Miller Documents: figs. 154, 157; Henry E. Peach: fig. 231;
Luigi Pellettieri: fig. 73; P. Rocheleau: fig. 235; Hugh Smeizer: figs. 9, 43–44,
63, 103, 229–30; Taylor & Dull: figs. 91, 184, 187, 193; Paul Warchol: fig. 241;
Delmore A. Wenzel: fig. 129; A. J. Wyatt, staff photographer: figs. 132, 168–69.

Edited by Gerald W. R. Ward
Designed by Ed Marquand with the assistance of
Vivian Larkins
This book was prepared for publication at Marquand Books,
Inc., Seattle
www.marquand.com

Library of Congress Cataloging-in-Publication Data
Kirk, John T.
    American furniture : understanding styles, construction,
and quality / John T. Kirk.
        p.   cm.
    Includes bibliographical references and index.
    ISBN 0-8109-4220-8 (hc: alk. paper)
    1. Furniture—United States. I. Title.
NK2405.K57 2000
749.213—dc21   00-27157

∞ The paper used in this publication meets the minimum
requirements of the American National Standard for Information Sciences—Permanence of Paper for Printed Library
Materials, ANSI Z39.48-1984.

Printed and bound in Hong Kong

Harry N. Abrams, Inc.
100 Fifth Avenue
New York, N.Y. 10011
www.abramsbooks.com